The Preacher's Library
Volume 4

Preaching in a Cultural Context

Martyn D Atkins

ISBN 1 85852 185 8

With thanks to God for Donald English,
who repeatedly reminded ordinary folk like me
how graciously, clearly and powerfully God
still speaks through preachers
whose lives and lips agree.

Martyn D Atkins is director of postgraduate studies at Cliff College, England, where he lectures on a number of topics including preaching, evangelism, missiology, and liturgy and worship. He is a Methodist minister, a Fellow of the College of Preachers, and a regular speaker at *Spring Harvest* and *Easter People.*

GENERAL INTRODUCTION

Preaching is a very particular form of communication which has always been important in the life of the Christian Church. At the beginning of the 21st century we are undergoing a revolution in the varieties, method and speed of our communications. Preachers of all denominations, ordained and lay, undertake this calling with an awareness that we preach in a changing context.

The Preacher's Library is designed to help us to think through, perhaps in some cases reassess, why we preach, how we preach, and to whom we preach. Some of the volumes in this series will take a fresh look at familiar issues, such as how preachers should approach various parts of the Bible, how we understand and express our doctrinal inheritance and the variety of styles in which preaching can be done. Other volumes will introduce issues which may be less familiar to many of us, such as the significance of our cultural context or the way in which the self-understanding of a woman preacher has important things to say to all preachers. Some of these books will offer direct help in the practice of preaching. Others will deal with issues which, although they appear more theoretical, impinge upon the preacher's task and on which we therefore need to have reflected if we are to preach with integrity in today's world.

All the writers in this series, lay and ordained, women and men, are recognised preachers within their own denominations and write with the needs of their colleagues firmly in mind. These books will avoid academic jargon, but they will not avoid dealing with difficult issues. They are offered to other preachers in the belief that as we deepen our thinking and hone our skills God's people will be blessed and built up to the glory of God.

In *Preaching in a Cultural Context*, Martyn Atkins tackles head-on some of the greatest challenges facing a contemporary preacher of the gospel. Whatever we make of what is sometimes called 'postmodernism', it is surely undeniable that the cultural and intellectual climate at the beginning of the 21st century is radically different from the one in which many of us have grown up. Our mental furniture is being changed. Many people now doubt whether 'big stories' (and Christianity is certainly that) are capable of being believed, whether there is such a thing as 'truth' (other than 'what works for me') and whether words can be used to point away from themselves to a reality they intend to describe.

This lucid, and at times passionate book, shows that we cannot ignore these challenges but contends that we must not be frightened of them. Martyn Atkins explores new ways of preaching the gospel in our cultural ferment, but warns that in order to do it effectively we may have to unlearn some things we thought we knew and begin to learn to preach differently.

Michael J Townsend

CONTENTS

1

BACK TO THE FUTURE

Like a rush of wind. Tongues of fire and strange languages. The promised Holy Spirit had come, the Church was born and the world would never be the same again. But Pentecost was not only about being blown away by blessing and bringing the Church to birth, it also made clear how God wanted the Church to communicate the gospel of Jesus Christ. Immediately these Jewish disciples are filled with the Spirit they begin to speak. They speak the praise and deeds of God. Not just in any old language but in each mother tongue of the Jews gathered from around the world. The crowd exclaims, in effect, 'They're speaking our language!' The ability to speak of God in other languages is the first gift of the Pentecostal Spirit.

It is significant that God chose to do it this way round. It would have been just as possible for God instantly to enable each person present to know a common language. It could have been a kind of ecstatic Esperanto. You know, Esperanto, the universal language spoken by . . . well, hardly anyone really. Which is probably why God chose another, better way. A key principle of gospel communication was being made clear from the outset. People need to hear the gospel in their own language, and they still do.

In response to the question 'What does all this mean?' Peter gets up to preach what was possibly his first sermon. Instinctively he seems to know some of the timeless lessons of gospel communication. For a start he begins by answering the question his hearers pose. Anyone who has rung a large company and encountered an 'electronic voice' will know how important that is. 'We are not drunk,' Peter says, 'and what you have witnessed means this . . .' He begins with their agenda, not his own.

Just *how* Peter goes about answering the crowd's question is also worth noting. He quotes passages from the prophet Joel and tells stories about Great King David. Why? Because his hearers are Jews – by birth or conversion – and as Jews, wherever they came from, would know such prophecies and stories. Recent discoveries suggest that the kind of 'last days' prophecies like Joel's were extremely popular among Jews at the time. Both these strategies – answering his hearer's questions and using material familiar to them and authorities accepted by them to do so – are valuable models of communication in the past and future alike.

But Peter doesn't just tell them what they want to hear. Some hard facts of faith are included. His sermon has a sting in the tail. He moves from being 'culture friendly' to being 'counter-cultural': 'This same Jesus who you crucified is both Lord and Christ,' he tells them. This was a great stumbling block for Jews. How can Messiah be crucified and die – a criminal's death at that? God would never permit it. But Jesus has died and so, to their mind, can't be Messiah. In this instance (even in Acts, preaching is not always so successful) Peter's words are received by the crowd, he suggests an appropriate (physical) response for those who repent and believe, and the membership figures of the First Christian Church, Jerusalem, go through the roof.

Peter is not unique in this respect. The preaching of Paul also reveals the same kind of culturally sensitive, culture challenging qualities. In Athens – centre of the ancient Greek world – for example, which was in many ways on a different planet to Jerusalem, Paul responds with great sensitivity to this very different cultural context. The account of his sermon in Acts 17 gives the impression that he has looked, listened, learned and lived among his hearers a little while before he speaks, which he does following an invitation by some local folk. He uses their statue to an unknown God as his starting point. Rather than attempting to demolish their (inadequate) spirituality he affirms them as religious people, seekers after truth. Given that Paul is a Jew – a law-upholding Pharisee at that – and knowing the deep Jewish hostility towards idolatry of any sort, this is remarkable. He also 'speaks their language', deliberately choosing a common, widely accepted style of public rhetoric and developing his sermon using a recognised form of logic. Jewish scriptures and concepts are not included – what is the point of quoting Jewish prophets if the Greek hearers all say, 'Joel who?' Instead he quotes from their own writings and poets, well-known mental furniture for those in front of him. Greek truth is presented in a Christian sermon. Paul is, after all, the great apostle to the Gentiles and Gentiles are different to Jews. All these responses are just right for this cultural context.

But Paul, like Peter, pulls no punches. He knows the stumbling block for his Greek hearers is the concept of the resurrection from the dead. Does he avoid it? Quite the reverse; this gospel theme is the very heart of his sermon. The response to his preaching is less numerically spectacular than in Jerusalem but is a proper one. Some laugh and walk away. Others say, 'We'd like to hear you again about this.' Such will always be the response to declarations of the Christian gospel.

The story of Paul before Felix, Festus and Agrippa in Acts 24-26 illustrates yet another culturally appropriate style of proclaiming the gospel. Here, in a formal Roman setting Paul uses neither Old Testament prophecies nor Greek poetry. But he does offer personal testimony to his faith and uses a recognised style of rhetoric and defence, absolutely appropriate for legal contexts such as this.

We are not limited to accounts in the Acts when demonstrating the profound cultural awareness of the earliest Christian preachers. It is widely accepted that the gospels themselves were shaped by the needs of those who produced them and those for whom they were produced. In a very real sense the gospels are 'preached sermons' before they are 'scripture'. Oral material precedes written material. Different cultural contexts are one reason why Jesus is presented differently in each gospel. For example, John's gospel is a carefully crafted attempt to proclaim the gospel using the language and images of pagan religions – the social-religious culture in which John and his community lived. But here, too, there is no fudging of the counter-cultural gospel. To those deeply sceptical about God appearing on earth, in human form, he declares 'And the Word became flesh and dwelt among us'. Dynamite! The use of *kurios* – Lord – as an alternative term to Messiah, picking up some of its themes yet also making it clear who Jesus was in a way understandable to Gentiles, was a stroke of culturally sensitive genius on the part of New Testament writers. As was, in a different way, the translating of oral Aramaic into written Greek, the common language of the time. The evidence piles up. From the very beginnings of Christianity, preaching has been about proclaiming the gospel *in a cultural context*. Christian preachers have always been about the business of preaching the gospel to those in front of them using 'tools' arising out of the wider prevailing culture.

The cultural sensitivity of apostolic preaching can be too easily overlooked. At least since C H Dodd's *The Apostolic Preaching and its Developments*, a classic text for preachers since its publication in 1936, there has been a tendency to focus upon the *unity and consistency* of apostolic preaching rather than its responsiveness to context. Dodd's thesis – that apostolic preaching employs the same handful of gospel themes (known as the *kerygma)* resulting in a 'common gospel' being proclaimed – has become widely accepted. Without rejecting that notion I note that the *emphasis, ordering and interpretation* of kerygmatic preaching is in fact highly culturally sensitive.

4

To reduce such cultural sensitivity to talk of mere strategy is to miss the point. Peter and Paul do not butter people up before going for the jugular. This is not some slick trick, an inauthentic first-century sales pitch. Nor is it the 'Mary Poppins' method – a spoonful of sugar makes the (gospel) medicine go down in a most delightful way! Peter and Paul begin with the agenda of those in front of them and go on to present sharp aspects of the gospel message to their hearers because they believe the gospel and believe it is good news. Their sermons always end up focusing upon Jesus Christ because he is for them the clue to all meaning, the lens through which life, the universe and everything makes sense. In order to answer the questions posed to them they *have* to preach the gospel of Jesus. This is the lasting value and significance of Dodd's book, for although apostolic preaching is more versatile and creative than he acknowledged, the crucial point that the gospel does possess a recognised shape and content is hammered home. In apostolic preaching different contexts produce different gospel emphases, the presentation of content changes, analogies alter and thought forms are transposed into other keys, but there remains an identifiable gospel, what Michael Green calls 'some sort of pattern of sound words'[1].

These are helpful parameters for preachers at the beginning of the third Christian millennium just as they have been for the previous two. There is a gospel to proclaim and creativity, imagination and sensitivity are required to proclaim it in every time and place. Preaching the gospel in every cultural context is fundamentally about joining God's Holy Spirit in the work of enabling every living soul to hear the good news of Jesus Christ in their own language.

When preachers recognise they are not in a strait-jacket on the one hand, and cannot just make it up as they go along on the other, the task of preaching in a cultural context is not ending as much as beginning. Just *how* the gospel is interpreted and applied in each time and place, *which* themes are most useful and relevant in a given situation, and at what point you might part company with the gospel is a dilemma which every Christian preacher has wrestled with, and been thrown, many times. As P T Forsyth put it in another classic book for preachers, *Positive Preaching and the Modern Mind*: 'We must all preach *to* our age, but woe to us if it is our age we preach, and only hold up the mirror to the time.'[2] Preaching the gospel, mindful of the broad cultural context in which this preaching takes place, is the main theme of this short book.

2

BALANCING

H e stood outside the Christian bookshop in the drizzle, the archetypal cartoon figure of ridicule. His sandwich-board proclaimed: 'Repent! The end of the world is nigh.' He preached love like some speak hate and never quite looked his small, largely mobile audience in the eye. But it probably didn't matter that few stood around; the sermon was the same whether or not anyone was present to hear it. Then I saw it, over the preacher's shoulder, in the bookshop window, and it made me smile. A poster, colourful and bright and clashing with the message of the sandwich-board: 'The earth is the Lord's, and everything in it.'

How preachers regard their cultural context in relation to the gospel determines what and how they preach. A preacher who views 'the world' as evil and corrupt preaches quite differently to the one who believes that 'the earth is the Lord's and everything in it'. One preacher sees the Church as a refuge in which people escape the prevailing culture; for another the Church is the launching pad for engagement in it. One asserts that being 'saved' entails coming out of the surrounding cultural context while another exhorts us to find salvation through service in it. Christians understand 'the world', the 'cultural context' and 'the gospel' quite differently, and the difference is often made crystal clear when they preach. A gospel that does not speak into any and every cultural context can't properly be gospel. A gospel that merely provides what any and every culture's itching ears long to hear can't properly be gospel. Preaching the gospel of Christ in any and every cultural context, then, is a balancing act. Christian preachers can't opt out and mustn't fall in.

To be a Pilgrim?

One helpful way of looking at the relationship between Christianity and its broad cultural context is suggested by Andrew Walls who sees the whole of Christian history in terms of a constant tension between two gospel principles.[1] The first principle he calls the 'Indigenous Principle'. This is the urge to live as a Christian in society, in the world. After all, God, through Christ, accepts us as we are and 'as we are' means people conditioned by a time and place, by language and customs, by family, group relations and wider society – in short, by 'culture'. As Louis Luzbetak puts it, 'Whenever God deals with human beings . . . he deals with them *as* cultural beings.'[2] How else could it be?

Without doubt the most powerful argument for this profound identification with the world is that it is just what God did in Christ. As a paraphrase of John 1:14 puts it, 'The Word became flesh and blood and moved into the neighbourhood.' We call it incarnation and it is of the very essence of the Christian gospel. Shouting by megaphone from heaven is not God's way. Becoming an extraterrestrial is not God's way. God's way is the indigenous way. So in order to redeem humanity the divine Word becomes a human being. The Lord of eternity has a human mother, is raised in a Jewish family in a backwater of the Roman Empire, eats the food, breathes the air and speaks the language of a first-century Jew. Jesus Christ becoming human is at the heart of all Christian engagement with culture, for if God adapted to human culture, then we can, and must. Even on the cross, Jesus Christ is supremely identifying with the world. Whenever the Church realises that it can't declare God's redeeming work in the world by isolating itself from the surrounding culture it adopts the Indigenous Principle. Whenever the Church imitates God – who in Christ makes his home in the world and in the Spirit works innovatively in every cultural context – it embodies the Indigenous Principle.

Then there is the second principle – the 'Pilgrim Principle'. This is the realisation that, in the words of the Negro spiritual, 'this world is not my home, I'm just passing through'. A Pilgrim rendition of John 1:14 reminds us that the divine Word came and 'tabernacled' among us for a while. For Christians, earth, for all its beauty and delight, is always going to be a temporary dwelling place. That is why Paul refers to our bodies as 'tents'. We are God's refugee people and our true citizenship lies in heaven.[3] God does call people, as they are, but then invariably transforms them. Becoming Christian is essentially about all things becoming new. In every generation, in each culture, therefore, Christians become aware that to follow Christ is to walk out of step with society, with the world, with the prevailing culture. It is to march to a different drum and a different drummer. No society on earth can absorb the gospel of Christ painlessly into its system because, ultimately, the kingdom of God is not of this world.

It is, of course, never all or nothing, never entirely Indigenous or Pilgrim. Hence the balancing act. Over history, however, and in response to different cultural contexts Christians have focused upon one principle more than the other. Were we to play snippets of the 'video' of Christian history this would become clear . . .

'Videoclip' One – An Apostolic Model
Date: *100-180CE*
Location: *A number of cities, towns and villages in the Roman Empire*

Pilgrim characteristics abound. It is a time of religious pluralism and Christians witness to their faith in a society of many different belief systems. The return of Christ is believed to be imminent, The End expected any moment. There is anticipation in the air. Ridicule, slander and persecution are common. Many Christians deal regularly with cruel laughter, false accusation and verbal bullying.

More seriously, Christians are regarded as a politically subversive force by the powerful ones of the day and because of that some terrible tales are told in the fellowship. Every Christian group knows someone imprisoned and can name martyrs. As we watch we witness tears, faith and joy in equal measure. It is clear that to become Christian is costly in many ways and offers little in the way of worldly benefits. Prayer and practical support for each other are vital and freely offered. As is often the case when backs are against the wall, local Christian communities are clearly deeply committed to each other, and yet do not appear 'cliquey' or introverted. Indeed despite all the drawbacks and limitations these churches are on a mission and many are growing. Everyday relationships are the means by which these Christians, many of them women, spread the message of the gospel.

Preaching and preachers . . .

Preaching in this cultural context is varied and the videoclip identifies several types of preaching going on in several contexts. Preaching is certainly *evangelistic*. Itinerant preachers call people to believe and follow Jesus Christ. They are a loosely-defined group of folk, coming and going, some known, some not. Some are highly effective, often having the greatest success among 'simple' folk, those considered the dregs of society by the powers that be – hence the ridicule and slander. Becoming Christian is about joining an alternative society.

Preaching is also *instructive*, and the role of the 'teacher-preacher' – often a member of the congregation meeting people in small groups – is clearly very important. Those becoming Christian are pagans and need a lot of schooling in the faith. They need to learn how to become disciples of Jesus Christ, how to move from darkness into Light. It takes time. Everyone works on the basis that the decision to become Christian is the beginning of a process, not its end. Only when a person knows what they are letting themselves in for as it were, and becomes baptised – a great occasion – are they regarded a 'Christian'. Until then they are 'seekers' and preaching is a key tool in helping them find what they seek.

Preaching is also *pastoral* and *practical*, and the 'pastor-preacher' is another vital figure (no doubt often one and the same as the teacher-preacher). Those experiencing persecution need strengthening. Those struggling need encouragement. The sacrificial lifestyle lived out by so many is sustained by preaching. The role of unsung preachers who, against some mighty odds, nurture tiny congregations in a growing Christian Church to the point where it will become the official religion of the Roman Empire, cannot be overstated.

Another thing emerges from the videoclip. Whether geared towards evangelism, instruction or pastoral care, preaching is *dialogical*. Interruptions and challenges arise all the time in the course of public speaking and nobody bats an eyelid. When Christian preachers contend for the faith in public interruptions regularly occur. It seems to be all part of the listening and responding model which has been a trait of Christian preaching since the time of the apostles. Paul uses a word implying dialogue rather than monologue to describe his preaching. 'What shall we do?' the Pentecost crowd asked Peter.

Preaching to Christians or seekers in training for baptism also involves dialogue. Questions are posed and clarifications sought from the preacher by the group and from the group by the preacher. The Latin word lying behind 'sermon' effectively means 'conversation', and so it often appears to be, even when only one voice is speaking. In this context dialogue is not heckling but rather engagement, clarification and affirmation. Sometimes the questioning happens during the sermon, sometimes afterwards. Either way it is clear that preaching – both outside and inside the Christian community - is essentially dialogical. The era when the preacher is considered six feet above contradiction and congregations sit in passive genteel silence is some way further on the videotape.

Why spend so much time looking at this part of the story? Well, this part of the Christian story is rightly very popular today. Western Christians are noting increasing similarities between this early period of Christianity and the present day. How Christians went about being Christians, making Christians and growing Christians in this pluralist setting, with limited social power and influence has clear and increasing relevance in a postmodern, post-Christian society. Indeed, some consider that the current cultural climate has more in common with that of the early Church than any time for 1,700 years. If so, then the models of preaching in that cultural environment may well have lessons to teach us today. Indeed, we might already have noted some!

'Videoclip' Two – A Christendom Model

Date: 350-460CE
Location: *A number of cities, towns and villages in the Roman Empire*

The Roman Empire has become officially Christian! Who would have thought it? Emperor Constantine's decision that the Empire adopt Christianity is, whichever way you look at it, a great victory, a testimony to the preaching, witness and martyrdom of countless Christians over nearly 300 years. If the book of Acts deliberately ends with Paul in Rome, awaiting an audience with the Roman Emperor in order to share the gospel with him, then the conversion of the Roman Empire represents the aim and climax of the story. The Christian faith has conquered the known world! Now millions will worship Christ. Now the Church can live and witness freely. Now a whole society, a whole culture, can be structured according to the Christian faith. Wonderful!

But the videotape tells of another side to all this, the price of success. Almost by definition everyone is now Christian, but what does it cost and what does it mean? The intensity we witnessed earlier has largely gone. Christianity appears less radically life-changing and more moderately life-enhancing. Faith for many appears superficial and nominal. Now we watch Bishops preach to thousands then stretch out their hands over the crowd and declare them to be Christian. Compared to the earlier days, when it had cost such a great deal and taken so long to become baptised this seems a 'pot-noodle' kind of Christianity – just add water and wait two minutes! We see preachers declare Caesar Lord on earth and Christ Lord in heaven, and after so many Christians gave their lives rather than swear such allegiance. We hear preachers urging Christians to fight the enemies of Rome and defend the Empire, when previous generations of the faithful had been so profoundly pacifist. The Church has gone 'into all the world', but it also appears that the world has come into the Church. In embracing the Church had Constantine hugged it to death? Overall, Indigenous rather than Pilgrim themes are most evident.

Preaching and preachers . . .

In this new cultural setting the nature of preaching has changed radically. The wandering charismatic evangelist preacher has disappeared. Sad really, but inevitable in a society where everyone is regarded a believer until it's clear they aren't, rather than vice versa. Besides, congregations are now more settled and most have an authorised leader of their own. The 'teacher-preacher' is still much in evidence, but it all looks and 'feels' quite different to the earlier clip. It is more 'official'. All the preachers are now male and almost all ordained. Preachers, like the Church, now have social standing and influence. Laughter and ridicule have given way to deference and respect. Some preachers seem now to be imposed upon congregations rather than emerging naturally out of them. They 'come across' as educated spokesmen for the Church rather than equals ministering to their peers. They seem to dispense the faith to the faithful rather than discover it with them. Indeed, the Church is more the custodian of sound teaching rather than the fellowship of the faithful learning the faith.

There is less genuine dialogue too. Preachers do not seem to listen and respond to their hearers in the way their predecessors did. Now it is much more a case of simply stating the case. The pastor-preacher role has been similarly affected. In fact the role of pastoral care is bound up with that of teaching, correcting and regulating, and is now often undertaken by one person. One stark difference from the earlier clip is the attitude towards non-Christians, who are now regarded as those in *error* rather than those in *need* of the gospel, and are often treated accordingly. It seems as if preaching in general has become less like attractive persuasion and more like assertive prescription.

Why spend time on this part of the story? Well, in some form or other 'Christendom' – the alliance of Christianity with its social political context, forming a 'Christian culture' – has been an abiding feature of Christian history ever since the fourth century. However, increasing numbers of Christians today are suggesting that Christendom is past its sell-by date and is fast perishing. They contend that the arrival of a 'post-Christendom' cultural context is asking serious questions about this 'cosy' relationship with power and influence – and about the kind of preaching generally associated with it. Consequently the model of preaching in that cultural environment may well have salutary lessons for us today. Indeed, we might already have noted some!

'Videoclip' Three – A Pluralist Model
Date: *1910-1990CE*
Location: *A number of cities, towns and villages in the 'West'*

The world has changed! For a start we know it's round, not flat. Development and discovery affect every area of human life – and beyond it. The Church too has altered dramatically. Previously a pretty varied institution but essentially 'One' it has now fragmented into hundreds of bits. It is as if someone has dropped a glass vase on a hard floor and we see certain colours and images reflected in the shards. Human beings themselves are changed. Not only are they stronger and longer living but reading, writing and thinking are taken for granted. They make decisions that profoundly affect their own lives, choosing to do this, to believe that, to reject the

other.   Such self-determining individualism is very
different to the patriarchal dependency culture so evident
in the earlier clips. Indeed, so radical are the changes to
people, Church and culture that we can be excused for
checking it's the same videotape!   Compared to the
previous clips it's almost like sci-fi.   Yet there are
similarities, vestiges of the Christianity of the previous
clips that reassure us it is essentially the same faith. Basic
components are identifiable (for example, a focus on Jesus
Christ, the use of certain scriptures, some core beliefs and
practices – including preaching – some form or other of
Church etc).   But each of these is altered from past
versions as we witness the effects of an incarnational
religion responding to an ever-changing cultural climate.

Like all previous generations of Christian people
these, living in 'the West' in the 20th century, are relating
their Christian faith to the world in which they live, their
macro-cultural context.   It is clearly a time of mixed
feelings and fortunes. There is some optimism around.
After all, Christianity is a living world faith. It is nearly
two millennia old. It has survived. More than that it has
profoundly affected some societies in terms of law,
morality, education, welfare and the like.   Stories of
revivals and missions are well-rehearsed, as are brave
tales of the expansion and numerical growth that have
taken place in many parts of the globe, though – and they
are acutely aware of this fact – not so much in their own
Western back yard.

More common than optimism, however, is realism, or
even pessimism. Overall, despite huge improvements in
almost every aspect of the standard of human living, it
appears that being Christian in the 20th century is, in many
ways, much more of a struggle than was the case in the
previous clip. The cultural wind is turning increasingly
chilly as we watch. There is very little open persecution,
so evident in some apostolic times, but there is
increasingly incredulity and ridicule. Hard questions and
challenges face the Church. If the previous clip (and an
awful lot of videotape after it) was about a Church 'in
charge' it now seems much less so. Impressions of power

and influence remain, but bubbling under the surface is a Christian Church most definitely on the 'back foot'. Bullets come from many directions, from other ideologies like Marxism and humanism, from capitalism, industrialisation and urbanisation, from a whole raft of modern sciences that seem to be very influential, and from certain philosophers and historians. All are posing searching questions to Christian faith. The nature of God, the true origins of the universe, humanity, goodness and ethics, the best shape for society, whether miracles actually happen, who really wrote the Bible – these, and hundreds more such questions are in the melting pot. Astute watchers realise that Christianity is back in a pluralist context, a faith in a sea of beliefs. It is, of course, a different sort of pluralism from the apostolic age (for example, one group believes that there is no God at all) but similarities are not hard to find. The prevailing western culture, in many ways itself a product of Christianity, is now weighing Christian faith in the balances and finding it wanting. Its relevance, its plausibility is under question. In the fastest-changing century in human history so far, western Christianity is becoming increasingly culturally sidelined.

Preaching and preachers . . .

A bewildering variety of preaching goes on in this exciting, challenging cultural context. We witness the return of the itinerant preacher-evangelist. He (and it remains mainly he) is still coming and going, often preaching from the edge of the Church and calling folk to follow Jesus. This call to discipleship tends to focus on mental assent to certain beliefs rather than calls to begin the demanding and lengthy process of becoming Christian we saw in much earlier times. Being saved seems to be more an 'inner' thing rather than an 'outer' thing. Indeed, joining the Church seems to be a relatively brief and easy business and in most cases seems not to necessitate those world-denying qualities we saw in the apostolic period. The nominality of the Christendom model is still much in evidence. Certainly there appears to be a general assumption that people know the Christian gospel and have rejected it rather than don't know it in the first place. So most preacher-evangelists call hearers *back* to faith. As the clip continues, however, and the 20th century moves into its final decades, we note that fewer and fewer potential hearers appear to have any real knowledge of faith to which to return.

Most 20th century preaching, however, is not undertaken by the itinerant preacher-evangelist, but by the official representative of the Christian Church. The similarities to the Christendom model are unmistakable. The official preacher continues to teach the faith and pastor the flock, though we note that now he (and it is still mainly 'he', though this is breaking down in certain churches) is now not, as was almost always the case previously, the most educated person in the congregation. We also notice that increasing numbers of non-ordained people are preaching in all kinds of churches.

The preaching of official representatives, both ordained and lay, is itself very diverse. There are genuine attempts at dialogue (some suggest this is the only model of sermon worth the candle) but many feel that nobody is really listening any more, or if they are that it is extremely difficult to find a common language for understanding each other. Pessimists are in evidence, preachers deeply sceptical about the world and locating the hope of a new heaven and a new earth in the belief that Christ will come again. They hint darkly at the possible extinction of the Church but disagree what to do about it. Some simply suggest surrender, others urge the Church to batten down the hatches, and stress faithfulness, purity and isolation in their sermons, while others urge taking the bull by the horns and engaging in evangelism in order to recapture the halcyon days so much loved and longed for. A bewildering variety of realist preachers are in evidence, each trying to respond to the challenges and opportunities of the age. One group preaches that in a world where biblical miracles are not popular cultural currency any more Christianity is, essentially, about loving your neighbour. Goodness knows, they say, after some of the wars of the century, what better expression of the Faith can there be? Indeed, many realist groups focus upon the human rather than divine aspects of religion – the 'horizontal' rather than 'vertical' dimensions of faith. These, and many subgroups besides, create a huge flux of Indigenous and Pilgrim themes flowing from the pulpits of 20th century Western Europe. Perhaps you have already recognised preaching colleagues and friends?

Why spend time on this part of the story? Because it is the immediate past, and its legacy remains strong. Western Christians today do not live in a state of total cultural novelty but in a state of 'inbetweenness'. Despite some claims about its inherent newness, our emerging 'postmodern' cultural context has not emerged *ex nihilo* – out of nothing. There is not radical cultural discontinuity at every hand. Most preachers – and most of their congregations – live in the twilight zone, a place somewhere in between the modern and postmodern understandings of life, the universe and everything. Consequently most preachers will continue to recognise in this sketchy outline of the recent past some features of the present cultural context in which they preach.

This said, there is undoubtedly a major cultural change in process in the West, many say as profound and far-reaching in its implications for Christianity as any in Christian history. The usefulness of sketching the contours of the recent past lies not only in noting continuity but also in identifying the extent and rate of cultural change currently going on. To look at where we were not so long ago is to become aware of what is changing fast and what is changing faster.

Insights for the way ahead

As we turn to the subject of preaching in the contemporary Western cultural context we can note some insights that have arisen out of the first chapters. These will be the working guidelines as we examine preaching in what many refer to as a postmodern context.

- The broad cultural context profoundly affects the nature of Christianity. It always has, and will continue to do so in a postmodern context. Cultural neutrality is therefore impossible; even to be counter-cultural is to be culturally influenced. Christians cannot choose *whether* to respond to the prevailing culture, but can choose *how* they will respond to it. They cannot escape from it but can capitulate to it, alter or transform it. They can decide whether to adopt Pilgrim or Indigenous stances in relation to aspects of the prevailing cultural context.

- Christian *preaching* is profoundly affected by the cultural context. Phillips Brooks said, 'Preaching in every age follows, to a certain extent, the changes which come to all literature and life.'[4] How a person understands the gospel, the world and the Church profoundly affects how they preach and what they preach. 'Hell fire and damnation', we are told, is a less popular and preached theme today than it was 200 years ago. No doubt some Christians have ceased to believe in it while others bitterly regret they have, but the perception of judgement and hell is profoundly connected to the nature of the prevailing culture (as is all Christian doctrine). Moral issues that express and define Christian faith and discipleship also change in line with cultural trends: temperance in that era, the cancelling of third world debt in this. Political correctness and inclusive language for God are, whatever else they are, religious examples of cultural sensitivity today. The music of much contemporary Christian worship uses rhythms, styles and language arising from 'secular' music and did not arise – some would say could not have arisen – prior to the 1960s.

- The relationship between preaching and culture can – and should – be put more positively. Christian preaching is not simply shaped by culture, like inert clay. It is required, even impelled, to engage with culture and seek to shape culture because of the nature of the gospel. The desire to communicate the gospel to those in front of you does not end with Peter and Paul; it is the aim of Christian preachers down the centuries, and this very aim means taking the surrounding culture seriously.

- Preaching in any cultural context, therefore, requires balance. It holds in tension gospel and culture, Indigenous and Pilgrim themes. The gospel of Jesus Christ is both culture-friendly and counter-cultural in any given setting. The preacher is the one called by God to watch, listen and speak, engage and define, affirm and challenge. In this way the offer of the gospel is made. The gospel offered is itself shaped by the cultural context, but also critiques the cultural context. As an advocate of the gospel of Jesus Christ the preacher speaks into and out of the prevailing cultural context. In a postmodern context, as in all cultural contexts, this is the great challenge and enormous privilege of Christian preaching.

3

LOOKING AND LISTENING

'The cultural gap between a forty-something parent and their teenage child,' said the speaker, 'is greater than the cultural gap between the parent and the 18th century Evangelical Revival.' 'A gross overstatement, surely?' was my first response. On reflection I'm not quite so sure, but then I'm a forty-something year old parent with teenage children!

Postmodernity

Whether or not the speaker's comment was 'over the top' we in the West are currently living through a huge culture shift. About this, there is little dispute. Of what this culture shift consists and what it means there is continuing and seemingly endless dispute. A common catch-all term for the culture shift is 'postmodern'; its philosophical, intellectual aspects are often referred to as 'postmodern*ism*', and its broader social and cultural aspects as 'postmodern*ity*'. Such terms will be new to some and already 'boo' words to others. The material here is designed mainly for the first group, for those, as yet, without much of a clue. As preaching in any and every culture is a balancing act then we must begin, as the early preachers did, by looking at and listening to our contemporary cultural context.

Our concern here is more with postmodernity than postmodernism, though like all such distinctions it shouldn't be pushed too hard. This doesn't mean that 'philosophical' themes – 'isms' – are absent, simply that the task of sketching out some themes of contemporary culture makes postmodernity a more appropriate term. After all, it is generally agreed that the term 'postmodern' first emerged from fine arts and architecture rather than academia. In fact some now argue that The Academy no longer directs the intellectual climate of culture as much as reflects it. Postmoder*nity* then, sets the arguments of The Academy within the wider context of contemporary culture, what Michael Paul Gallagher calls 'postmodernity of the street'[1]. That is the focus here. It is a wide focus. Everything that makes up the diverse landscape of our cultural context is welcome at the table: as we shall see, postmodernity loves plurality. Notions of 'high' or 'low' culture are rejected as old hat, creations of the 'modern' age, an age dominated by authorities and elitism that postmodernity is eager to reject. So Pavarotti sings at football matches and eminent academics appear on silly chat shows. Film maker Steven Spielberg and Microsoft's Bill Gates, as much as philosophers like Derrida and Lyotard, are the movers and shakers, the prophets of postmodernity. There is no 'high' or 'low' culture, only a cultural smorgasbord from which to choose: as we shall see, postmodernity loves choice. I mean, why have four TV channels, when you can have 400? Consequently what is under discussion here is not merely of interest to 'anoraks' and traditional academics in their proverbial ivory towers. Reading the runes of our culture through the lens of our Christian faith, and acting Christianly in response to what has been 'read' is now an essential rather than optional requirement of those in leadership roles in the local church.

Natives and non-natives

But if the speaker above is even half-right there is a real question whether or not a forty-something year old is the right person to pronounce about postmodernity at all, indeed, whether they *can*. In some senses my (three very different) teenage children would do it much better though it is unlikely their attempt would involve writing much at all (postmodernity is more visual, oral, aural and tactile than literary). For them a *book* about preaching in a postmodern context is a no-no for a start; it's like using a bottle opener to peel a banana! They seem to accept postmodernity like the law of gravity. They no longer hear the clock ticking (many of their timepieces don't tick anyway); postmodernity is just the way things are. Theirs is a postmodern 'worldview'. (That's how you think about the world when you're not really thinking about it, your frame of reference for understanding the world in which you live.) Even though they each belong to quite different youth sub-cultures ('tribes', Pete Ward calls them) they accept postmodern themes as normal. To them postmodernity is . . . (to use a phrase of Graham Cray) '. . . Well, s'obvious, innit!' They know no other cultural environment. It is their 'default' position and they understand it in terms I never will no matter how hard I try.

And yet chronologically challenged forty, sixty and ninety-something year olds can identify postmodern themes and offer comment on them. Indeed, it is quite important that they do. 'Oldies' will never 'know' postmodernity like its 'natives' do, but an inevitable by-product of being a little longer in the tooth is that they have witnessed more of the continuing deconstruction of the old and construction of the new. Unlike the natives, non-natives are able to place postmodernity in the context of something else. Postmodernity may not be the 'oldies' default position. In cultural terms we may spend our time converting pounds, shillings and pence into decimal coinage. While our children or grandchildren sit fearlessly at a PC we may cower before a computer nervously reading the manual. But the plain fact is that whereas it may not be our native air *it is still the air we breathe*, and increasingly so. Postmodernity is becoming the dominant cultural worldview of our society and as such it affects us all. In this sense we are children of our contemporary culture whatever our age. The subcultures in Western society today are bewilderingly diverse, but at a macro cultural level we are all breathing the same air and that is the complex air of postmodernity.

A call to conversion

I make here then (rather than at the end) a call to conversion! It is vital that Christian preachers recognise the pervasiveness of postmodernity, take it seriously and engage with it and reflect upon it, not least in terms of their preaching. Not to do so will allow some to perpetuate the myth that it doesn't concern them or affect the Church and that would be disastrous. Waiting for 1954 to come round again is not the answer! Mr 'I'm 56 and can't be expected to understand all this stuff' and young Ms 'There's nobody in my congregation under 60 so what's the point?' miss the point. The postmodern thing is not, in the end, an ageist issue. It pervades our lives, our churches, and our congregations, from the baby about to be baptised to her nonagenarian great, great-grandmother. Ask anyone of any age; the word on the streets – not just the ivory towers – is that the world has changed. Even those on the back row with their hearing aids turned off, while flatly refusing to plug into the loop system, know the basic truth of postmodernity – the world isn't like it used to be. If preaching is offering the gospel to those in front of us, then *all* those in front of us - including ourselves - are increasingly affected by postmodernity. It is radical in that it affects the way we 'know' and 'understand' our culture. As such it cannot be uncritically accepted or thoughtlessly dismissed. A basic contention of this book is that postmodernity is neither the pit of hell nor the new Jerusalem, but simply the present broad cultural context in which Christian preachers are called to offer the gospel of Jesus Christ. As in a pre-modern era, so in a postmodern one: looking and listening in order to speak out of and into the prevailing culture, is the order of the day.

A betwixt and between way forward

OK, so we're willing to look and listen and learn, and because we're still reading a text we're probably non-natives in this postmodern culture. Where do we start? We probably want to start with a crisp definition of the subject, followed by a coherent and comprehensive overview of it. A total picture would be built up. We'd have it sussed, sorted. That would suit us nicely. But we hit a problem immediately. This very approach is a *modern* way of treating *post*modern material and one of the more definite things that can be stated about *post*modernity is that it hangs loose to the ways of modernity. Besides, postmodernity dislikes and distrusts 'comprehensive overviews' of anything. It prefers variety, fragmentation, and even contradiction rather than logic or coherence. So the definition/comprehensive overview approach has its problems.

But we have to start somewhere and here we adopt a 'betwixt and between' approach. This means there is no attempt to try to 'explain' postmodernity in logical, coherent terms but nor are we going to revel in illogic and incoherence. It means the 'definition' question will be mooted but we will be content that postmodernity is currently impossible to define in hard and fast terms. It means some postmodern themes and traits will be identified but it won't matter that they lie uneasily with each other or present a fragmented, incomplete picture. This said, the following themes have not been chosen at random. There is method in the madness. The criteria for inclusion is not overall coherence, descending importance or unfolding logic, but is *that each chosen theme impacts the task of Christian preaching in some way.* Some of the ramifications of these postmodern themes for preaching and preachers will be flagged up in the next chapters. In this one we mainly come to the subject with open eyes and open ears. However, I encourage readers to stop every so often, grab a coffee, some wine or a whisky – whichever is your poison – and ponder on the implications and ramifications for your own faith and therefore your own preaching.

Jelly wrestling

Let's return to the definition question first. Those new to this whole postmodern thing quickly discover that it's very hard to pin down. This is hardly surprising. Catch-all terms tend to catch all manner of meaning. So some observe that 'postmodern' can mean almost anything you want it to mean, that it amounts to no more than the agreement of everyone in the room. Today anything new or reworked, profound or superficial, zany and 'off-the-wall' might be termed postmodern. It's like wrestling with a jelly. Postmodernity exults in fluidity not fixedness, relativity not regulation, diversity not definition. It's slippery. It's hard to get a handle on. It's replete with that 'Ah, but what about . . . ?' quality. Consequently it drives some folk nuts and delights others. In fact the level of frustration produced by such definition-fluidity is a good indicator of a person's postmodern friendliness, so readers can already engage in some self-assessment!

'Modern' and 'postmodern'

Yet the very term 'post*modern*' suggests a connection with 'modern'. We are not, after all, outlining themes of 'AbsoluteNewness' or 'TotallyUnlikeAnythingElseism', but postmodernity. This leads many to an essentially negative definition: Q. What is 'postmodern?' A. It is not 'modern'! Whatever 'modern' is, this comes after it. Postmodernity is, therefore, variously presented as a reaction to, or a rejection of, or a re-evaluation of some central themes of modernity. Modernity (an era which, for neatness rather than strict accuracy, is sometimes said to start in 1789 with the crumbling walls of the French Revolution and end in 1989 with the crumbling walls of Berlin) wallowed in the supremacy of human reason, postmodernity seems much less enamoured with such things. Modernity virtually came to worship the scientific method; (a product of human reason), whereas postmodernity is a nominal believer, a *user* of science and technology rather than a worshipper. Modernity was brash and confident that things would get better and better (a fruit of 'faith' in the scientific method), postmodernity tends to be sceptical and dismissive of such idealism. Modernity came to divide what it regarded as value-free facts (such as those provided by modern sciences) from value-laden private opinions (such as religious faith commitments); postmodernity makes much less of the division. In short, postmodernity puts a big question mark next to some of the main achievements of modernity. Although some presentations tend to make modernity more monolithic and 'wooden' than it probably was, in order to stress the fact that postmodernity is more fluid than it may be, the stance is clear: postmodernity is effectively 'late modernity', a reaction to the perceived exhaustion of modernity. This approach is beginning to change, however, as more and more postmodern 'natives' outline themes and theories without recourse to modernity which, for them, is as foreign as postmodernity is to 'oldies'. Postmodernity itself is currently under construction. Whether or not these different approaches will produce dramatically different versions of postmodernity, it is too soon to say; hence the impossibility and undesirability of hard and fast definitions.

Certainty not!

Postmodern culture tends to dislike and distrust talk of certainty. It has been suggested that a question mark is a good symbolic image for a postmodern approach to life. The distrust and dislike stems from a number of factors. One is the link between certainty and *arrogance*, a characteristic not highly regarded in many cultures and definitely not a postmodern one. The arrogance of certainty is regarded by some as not only offensive but also extremely *dangerous*. Isn't human history littered with the wretched legacies of those who were certain, arrogant and powerful? Doesn't certainty always lead to cultural crusades, to oppression and domination? As Zygmunt Bauman has stated hauntingly, 'Those who say they know the truth always go on to say in one way or another, therefore I must be obeyed.'[2] If so, a life free from eternal truths and certainties is a much better choice.

Another reason why certainty is disliked is the view that it tends to lead to *intolerance* and generally speaking, with a few notable – even quirky – exceptions, intolerance is something that postmodernity will not tolerate. To be certain about something also usually suggests that a person has broken faith with the givenness of relativism.

They have 'made their mind up' and thereby closed down options and rejected alternatives, whereas postmodernity prefers permanently keeping its options open, being perpetually provisional. There is also a general assumption that those who are certain about something are likely to be *wrong*. Life is so complex, issues so complicated, ideologies so provisional, surely anyone who is certain about anything just doesn't understand the real situation? The only thing you can be certain of is that you can't be certain about anything. A hint of simple naivety is, therefore, usually assumed to be lurking about in all declarations of certainty. Surely it must be, at the end of the day, the product of a limited mind and a stunted imagination? No wonder, then, that a postmodern cultural climate is generally dismissive towards those who claim certainties, especially in relation to beliefs and values.

Vive la différence!

Postmodernity not only welcomes cultural variety, diversity and plurality; it positively revels in it. Variety provides the messy cultural *mélange* from which the postmodern consumer exercises his or her right of choice. Just as a road full of restaurants offering cuisine from round the world can offer a richer, more interesting diet than Fred's café, so a plurality of ideologies provides a richer, more interesting community and a diverse, multi-faith presence produces a richer, more interesting society. As the manager of the new 'Tate Modern' in London put it, 'People no longer expect or want everything to be found in the same place.' Postmodernity takes it for granted that no single view of anything will be better than a collection of views. Not only that, no single view or belief is regarded as intrinsically more valid than the others. This leads to the often-noted 'pick n' mix' quality of postmodern culture. Much better that two people each listen to 2,000 radio stations of their own liking than 4,000 folk forced to listen to one station. As far as postmodernity is concerned à la carte is always better than table d'hôte.

Postmodern revelry in variety and diversity arises out of a rejection of 'big pictures', of full, fixed and final explanations of how the world is and how it can be understood. The technical term for these comprehensive accounts of 'life, the universe and everything' is 'metanarratives' – or 'big stories' – towards which, in a famous quote by Jean-Francois Lyotard, postmodernity expresses 'incredulity'. Put bluntly, postmodernity dislikes and disbelieves metanarratives (except perhaps the ones it appears to be constructing!). Metanarratives are disliked because they, like the certainty they produce, inevitably lead to oppression and dominance, they narrow down rather than open up choice, they restrict rather than liberate people. They are disbelieved because postmodernity is doubtful that there is any comprehensive and final explanation to be had anyway. Ideologies that try to account for and explain every question, every situation, or offer one central meaning for existence, are treated with great scepticism. Consequently not only is a metanarrative undesirable and limiting, it deceives by proposing the impossible. Postmodernity prefers fragmentation, micronarratives, mini-stories, especially our own stories about personal choices, multiple stories, any one of which is not required to relate logically to the others. So you can believe in God, disbelieve in the after-life, but believe in reincarnation. Inconsistent? So what! Who needs coherence, an overall explanation, and a big map? Such things belong to modernity. What a great postmodern symbol it was when the Berlin Wall came down and people went home with pieces of bricks and mortar!

Relatively speaking

Bubbling underneath postmodern wariness about certainty and the wallowing in variety are themes already noted in passing, but now requiring a little fuller treatment. Many features of postmodernity arise out of a prior commitment to pluralism and relativism. It is taken for granted that several opinions, viewpoints, truth claims, ideologies and the like, is a good thing. Let a thousand voices ring out! But, of course, in the face of quite different, even mutually exclusive, opinions, viewpoints, truth claims etc, the realisation quickly dawns that they cannot all be right. Consequently, rather than choose between them, or opt for any one, or adopt some criteria for who is right or wrong, what is true or false, postmodernity instead opts for the view that all such knowledge, belief, truth and the like, is relative. It proceeds on the assumption that there is no absolute reality or truth that determines the shape of everything else, everything is put on roller-skates! (Those sharp on the uptake have noted that if *everything* is relative, then relativity has become the only absolute!)

Using a story by G E Lessing, Roy Clements illustrated this developing understanding of pluralism and relativism to a conference on postmodernity. A man has three sons and a magic ring which, as he nears death, must be handed on to a chosen son. Not wishing to choose between his sons the father makes two other rings and, as he reaches his last days, gives each son a ring. On his death each son claims that he has the true ring and a squabble breaks out, so Nathan the Wise is called in to adjudicate. Unable to identify the true ring he delivers a classic judgement: let each son think and act as if their ring is the magic ring and in the meantime act towards each other with understanding and tolerance.

The story as it stands presents a 'late-modern' rather than 'postmodern' understanding of truth and reality. One of the rings is regarded 'truly' or 'really' magic and two are not. We cannot yet establish which is which but, given time, we will. Until then, tolerance and respect are requested. A belief that objective truth and reality exist and can and will be identified, permeates the story. Postmodernity rejects Nathan's theory and reasoning but retains the call for tolerance and respect. There is no real or true ring at all. Therefore, it would be much better to counsel the sons to believe that there is magic in all three rings, or better still that any magic resides more in the psychic act of believing than in the rings themselves! Postmodern pluralism and relativism is, therefore, of a more radical kind, a kind where the idea of absolute reality or objective truth is deemed at best irrelevant and at worst impossible. Reality and truth are not what they used to be.

What are words worth?

The postmodern commitment to and belief in relativism affects not only ideas and concepts, but also words and language. Given that preachers are wordsmiths the postmodern notion that language is relative is highly significant. According to postmodern thinking words and language have gone the same way as magic rings. It used to be assumed that words actually referred to real things, to objective things, to truth. The word 'God' was thought to refer to The Ultimate Reality. 'Chair' was thought actually to identify something you can sit on. Postmodernity rejects this and assumes instead that words and language are relative. Sure, they are necessary as tools of communication, but don't possess or connote 'reality' in any way. Consequently, as anyone with 'A' level English will have realised by now, postmodernity has gone big time into 'deconstruction'. In fact postmodern writers are in the vanguard of language deconstruction. Jacques Derrida, for example, rejects what he terms 'logocentrism' and asserts his belief that there is 'nothing outside the text' that is not shaped by the text. [3] 'A prison house of language' he calls it. Put starkly, language has no ultimate meaning and is, therefore, able to mean whatever the reader or user wants it to mean. You can only use words to unpack words. Words need more words, which need more words. But even when you have used up all the words in the world you have not gone outside words because they are 'self-referential'; they refer to nothing but themselves.

A personal Legoland

With its acceptance of radical pluralism (the welcome existence of several competing ideologies and their claims to truth) and relativism (the assumption that no ideology or truth claim is superior to any other), postmodernity embraces what Graham Cray calls 'constructivism'[4]. That is, we construct our own meaning and apart from our construction it is doubtful that meaning exists in any absolute sense. Like the reworking of the story of the rings we have moved away from the idea that truth exists and can be found, and towards the belief that we pick and choose, constructing what we feel we need to get by. Much contemporary spirituality is highly influenced by constructivism, as witnessed by an increased tendency to DIY, individualised faith. Constructivism also lies behind interactive computer games and television programmes. *The Face* magazine, in an 'Essay on the Nineties' put it like this: 'If it's the real thing we're wanting just where do we find it? The nineties' quest for life and some sort of authenticity coupled with a gradual loss of faith in the capacity of big beliefs to save our souls, has led us to make up our own truths, build our own small worlds as best we can.' Postmodernity is the cultural, philosophical, spiritual version of Legoland.

Knock knock, who's there?

The attempt to identify some basic descriptions of postmodern people is, of course, a very 'non-native' thing to do – a typically 'modernist' hankering after tidiness and coherence. Surely the whole idea of a commitment to relativism and constructivism means that there will be more exceptions than rules, that postmodern people will be unique, like their fingerprints? Maybe, maybe not. Presumably postmodern tolerance and relativism will permit that the reverse can be argued, that a common commitment to relativism and constructivism produces some basic images of the postmodern person. I proceed on this basis.

Shoppers and Consumers

Postmodern people can be described as shoppers and consumers. They construct their truth or 'identity' by picking and choosing this and that, and the ability to choose, change and choose again is the right and prerogative of the consumer. (Consumerism itself – and the capitalism lurking behind it – is rarely weighed in the balances by postmodernity.) Alongside René Descartes' famous Latin one-liner *cogito ergo sum* (I think therefore I am) goes *Tesco ergo sum* – I shop therefore I am.

Who to be, who not to be, that is the question . . .

Even personal identity becomes a matter of choice. Identity, for a 'modern' person came largely through what they *did* (that is, as a unit of production, paid or unpaid), whereas postmodern identity comes through exercising consumer choice. 'Who I am' has less to do with 'what I do' in terms of work and more to do with 'what I do' in terms of leisure. 'How I look' and 'how I feel' both relate to what I have chosen as a consumer. The *style* and *lifestyle* I choose identify who I am. Self-identity, then, is largely 'put on'. It is a social construct, and because consumerism requires both built-in obsolescence and constant make-over in order to work, self-identity can be – must be – constructed over and over again. How authentic these images are, whether there is anyone 'real' under the multiple masks is open to question and one of the heart-cries of postmodern people. As someone put it, 'You're born, you live, you run around a bit, you die. So you might as well look foxy while you're doing it!'

Living for today

No surprise, then, that 'now' is very important to postmodern people, far more so than 'was' or 'will be'. It has been said that modernity is characterised by a savings book and postmodernity by a credit card. Postmodern people think little of sacrificing now for some future benefits and much more highly of taking the waiting out of wanting. Freddie Mercury hit the right note: 'I want it all and I want it now.' Postmodernity is, therefore, ambivalent about history. The 'modernist' view that history is the key category for understanding existence is rejected. Postmodern culture is aware of history but, like so much else, invests it with no real authority. It borrows what it needs and adapts what it borrows, compressing history into the present and causing some to talk of the 'end' of history. The real value of history is to provide a wonderfully diverse variety of styles, practices and beliefs that can be uprooted and used in new personal constructions, rather than to guide or direct the present or the future.

Pragmatists

Postmodern people, then, are highly pragmatic. 'Does this work for me?' is a key criteria for accepting or rejecting all sorts of knowledge and information. Hence the postmodern impatience with the 'modern' division of the 'real facts' of science from the 'mere opinions' of faith. The postmodern person doesn't tend to dispute recent advances in the field of physics any more than new developments in theology. Both are subjected to the same filter system, the same sort of questions: 'Does it work for me? Does it resonate with my experiences?' If not, then whatever the merits of new science or new theology may be they are simply discarded. The constructor has no need of them and consequently they are deemed to be irrelevant. What a person knows and the ideas they have are, like history, not regarded as received wisdom as much as tools for living. Actions judge the merit and value of theories and ideas and not vice versa. If it works, it's good. If it makes sense of our experiences, it must be true.

Individual selves?

Common to all these images is an emphasis on the individual self. In one sense there is little to suggest that postmodernity is rejecting this bastion of modernist thinking. It still appears to be '*I* think, or shop, therefore *I* am', '*I* want it – now.' In fact, some suggest postmodernity may be intensifying the focus on the individual. For example, it has been noted that postmodernity has shifted significance away from the signified – the 'it' – and towards the signifier – the 'I'. In other words, the fact that *I* choose is more significant than *what* I choose. Others are not so sure, pointing out that postmodern individuals and 'modern' individuals seem very different. They talk about 'the death of man' as shorthand for a postmodern rejection of the central role modernity gave to individuals as conscious, individual, thinking, rational selves. The upshot of all this is that some regard postmodern people as optimistic, but many as essentially pessimistic. Some point to the swagger, others to a crippled inside. Is consumerism based on contentment or dissatisfaction? Does constructivism lead to freedom or rootlessness? Is permanently keeping your options open a signal of freedom or futility? Do multiple self-images make for sanity or schizophrenia? Is the focus on *now* an expression of hedonism or fatalism? Does disbelieving absolutes bring about liberty or lostness? Is 'pick n' mix' eclecticism an act of delight or despair? In short, has the postmodern person got it all together or are they falling apart? The jury is still out, but either way Christian preachers will rightly find it hard to believe that the gospel of Christ has nothing to offer such people.

Connected selves?

Alongside this continuing emphasis on the individual, however understood, and lying uneasily with it in many respects, is an acknowledged yearning for *connectedness*. Postmodern people do not, at the end of the day, care much for the radical loneliness of existential heroes. It is no accident that in a postmodern context the New Age concept of Gaia – the essential interconnectedness of everything – is a popular and powerful one. Technology in particular brings the world (and beyond) onto our TV and computer screens instantly. Yet the inter-connectedness of the Internet is not that of an African tribe, or a Welsh village when the pit was still open. For all its wonders global technology retains a 'you in your small corner and I in mine' quality. Therefore, the jury also remains out on the question of whether or not postmodern people are individual consumers meeting in common interest groups, or are profoundly committed to the notion of community (with its sublimation of the individual in favour of the collective).

'Spiritual' people

Finally, postmodern people can be described as spiritual people. 'Spiritual', rather than 'religious' as religion smacks of the authoritarian formalism and 'closedness' so much disliked. Most of the traits outlined above are brought into the choosing of 'some' – as much as 'a' – spirituality. Having rejected and put out of mind the possibility of a single, absolute source from which all spirituality takes its origin, postmodern spirituality is constructed by a consumer, who tastes, samples, accepts, rejects and changes in accordance with what they feel they need. Any historical rite or practice from around the globe is on the menu (except Christianity which, it is assumed – often wrongly – has already been tried and found wanting), the more exotic and esoteric the better. Hence the huge increase of Neo Pagan and New Age spirituality among postmodern Western people. Spirituality is plural and relative and better if it arises from a variety of sources. It often entails individuals 'into' certain kinds of spirituality coming together. And it must 'work', and work 'now'.

A postmodern worldview quite clearly sheds light and creates shadows and these contrasts are witnessed among postmodern people. Among natives and non-natives alike there is little claim that postmodernity is a panacea, promising world peace and harmony, the end of all evil, suffering and strife. Its rejection of such metanarratives and commitment to fragmentation makes it much more modest than that. There is little optimism about the future, ask around. But nor is there any desire to go back to the old ways; their authoritarianism and corruption have been weighed in the balances and been rightly rejected. Consequently, among shafts of light, among the glitz and hype and the ludicrous suggestions that every person can be what he or she wants to be, there is a deep heaviness about much postmodern thinking. Gasps of awe and sighs of despair often run together.

Second 'post'

Many today claim that Western society, particularly Western European society, is not only becoming increasingly postmodern but is also post-Christian. A common term to describe this (huge and diverse) theme is 'secularism' or the process of 'secularisation'. Whether or not secularisation is distinct from postmodernity, and if so how, and which is the chicken and which the egg, depends on which pundit you choose to listen to. The process of 'secularisation' almost certainly pre-dates 'postmodernity', but for our purposes their relationship is a sterile issue, as preaching in a contemporary context indisputably entails proclaiming the gospel to people profoundly influenced by both secularisation and postmodernity. 'Videoclip Three', in the previous chapter, contains some basic information about the process of secularisation.

There are probably as many versions of secularisation as there are sociologists of religion. The central theme however, is pretty well defined; Western societies and communities, previously identified and defined as 'Christian' in a variety of ways, have changed so as to be better identified and described as 'post-Christian' or 'secular'. Secularisation, then, marks the end of 'Christendom' (alive and well in 'Videoclip Two' and terminally ill in 'Videoclip Three' in the previous chapter) and the emergence of what might be termed a Western, post-Christian mission field. Grace Davie, in her book *Religion in Britain since 1945*, employs the shorthand phrase 'believing without belonging' to describe the religious situation of Great Britain at the end of the 20th century.[5] Her thesis presents a profound challenge to the Christian Church. Increasingly, (secular) people do not 'belong' to organised religious groupings – a fact plainly borne out each time the denomination in which I am an ordained minister, British Methodism, declares its membership figures! This exodus from the Churches is not, however, the result of mass atheism, as the growing body of unchurched people 'believe'. The key question then becomes 'believe what?' and the short version of the answer Davie supplies is 'all sorts of things' most of which do not fall within orthodox Christian faith. Another Sociologist of Religion, Steve Bruce, presents a more radical version of secularisation than Davie (and one offering less encouragement to formal Christian faith in contemporary Britain), but essentially confirms the view that secularisation has produced more unorthodox belief than out and out atheism[6]. Given that a central plank of the secular hypotheses of previous generations was 'the death of God', then the persistence of faith, in whatever forms, is itself significant, and represents a clear point of connection between postmodernity and secularism. That is, whether viewing contemporary society through the lens of 'postmodernity' or 'secularisation' it is agreed that most contemporary people are people of faith, or, put a better way, 'spiritual' people.

Spirituality is, of course, only one feature of 'secular' people. George Hunter III has spent over 30 years interviewing thousands of unchurched people in the US and the UK. In his book, *How To Reach Secular People*, he lists some key insights arising from his extensive research, all of which speak to preachers seeking to proclaim the Christian gospel in the contemporary cultural climate. Secular people:

- Are not a single homogeneous group, but diverse groupings.
- Vary in their consciousness of Christianity, including those with no Christian memory at all (Hunter calls these 'ignostics'); those with a very distant Christian memory ('notional Christians'); and those engaging in 'civil religion', the dry legacy of Christendom ('nominal Christians'). All but the last group – the nominals – are not 'churchbroke', that is, they don't know how to act, what to say or do in church.
- Have not been rendered 'religionless' by secularisation, but like consumers pick and choose off the religious à la carte menu.
- Have not been rendered 'immoral' by secularisation, but their morality is decreasingly shaped by Christian factors.
- Have rarely rejected the Christian case totally on rational grounds. In fact, most are not particularly sophisticated or as philosophically well-read as we tend to assume, and the beliefs they profess are more likely to have come from the school playground or a biology lesson than from an influential university professor friend whose loss of faith has 'rubbed off'.

Despite their diversity, Hunter asserts that most secular people share certain characteristics which, while broad generalisations, can be identified. For example:

- They are essentially ignorant of basic Christianity.
- They are 'life oriented' and, therefore, more interested in seeking life before death than after it. They are aware of their mortality but fear extinction more than they fear hell or seek heaven.
- They are more conscious of doubt than guilt.
- They have a negative image of the Christian Church. They doubt the intelligence, relevance and credibility of the Church – and its advocates.
- They have multiple alienations – from nature, neighbours, their work, economic and political systems and the like.
- They are untrusting. (Hunter follows Schuller in rejecting the notion that infants come into the world trusting and then learn to distrust, and adopts the idea that human beings enter life afflicted by a lack of trust that tends to intensify over time.)
- They have low self-esteem. Fundamentally they are self-centred and self-deceiving and deep down inside they know it.
- They experience history as out of control and feel that no one is 'in charge'. Consequently many face the future with anxiety.
- They experience things in their own life as 'out of control'. Sex, alcohol, money, hedonism, addictions from which they are powerless to free themselves and know in time will destroy them.
- They cannot find – or find it difficult to accept – a 'door', a 'way out'.[7]

In a not dissimilar exercise to George Hunter's, following some research in Birmingham, England, Martin Robinson drafted out *The Faith of the Unbeliever* in a book of that title. Following Davie and Hunter, Robinson affirmed that an 'unbeliever . . . is not someone who does not believe in God', but one 'who has chosen to step outside of the Christian tradition either to express an informal faith or to celebrate having no particular religious faith'.[8] Unbelievers, then, do not believe in nothing. They believe in an impersonal God – a life force rather than a personal being. They adhere to 'folk religion' – a mixture of superstition and religious traditions and beliefs of various types. They are generally indifferent towards the Church. Their beliefs rarely have any formal content and are generally used like fire extinguishers – for emergency use only. Unbelief is belief without belonging, which, in turn, leads to belief without content, and eventually belief without meaning.

Between these two 'posts' – postmodernity and post-Christianity – lies much of the landscape of contemporary society. In a general sense postmodern, post-Christian people are those 'in front of us', those to whom the gospel of Jesus Christ must be offered. In a more literal sense, however, they are the very people who are *not* 'in front of us' when we preach in church! Hence the earlier 'call to conversion' to which, true to my evangelical roots, I return now, at the end of this chapter. We preachers have a choice to make. We can pretend that our congregations are impervious to all this, a breed apart, and become – or remain – 'ghetto preachers'. Many congregations love such preachers even though this approach would appear to do neither them nor their preachers much good at all. Or we can recognise the pretence for what it is, a pretence that accounts in part for why there are so many Unbelievers and Ignostics out and about, but so few actually 'in front of us'. We can be honest and acknowledge that *we ourselves* are not 'teflon coated' in respect of the prevailing cultural climate. *We are* 'those in front of us' *as well as* those charged by Christ to live out the gospel in this cultural context with the special privilege of offering the gospel to all through the ministry of preaching. To realise this, to take it seriously, to let looking, listening and learning inform our faith and infuse our preaching, to speak the timeless good news of Jesus back into our culture in an attuned, sensitive and challenging way, is to begin to preach more effectively in our cultural context. And it is, of course, to adopt the approach of Peter and Paul.

4

GETTING ENGAGED

What do we make of it?

After a particularly fine 'eat all you can' buffet in a nice Indian restaurant, when we were 'full to bursting' having sampled a good number of the 37 dishes on offer, the smiling proprietor came over to our table and asked 'What did you make of it?' Our bland reply 'It was lovely' cut little ice. 'Which dishes in particular?' she wanted to know. What did we think of that dish . . . and why didn't we like the other? So we proceeded to dissect the buffet even as we were digesting it!

The remainder of this book deals with the same, initial question: postmodern, post-Christian culture: *what do we make of it*? Or, put another way, having 'looked', we now seek to engage with what we have looked at and apply appropriate insights to our preaching. Some readers will approach this prospect feeling not unlike I did at the end of the huge buffet! Surely any attempt to respond to every facet of postmodern, post-Christian culture included in the previous chapter would be a sure-fire recipe for severe indigestion? Thankfully we are spared such an attempt by coming at this mountain of material from a certain perspective. Our concern is 'what do we make of it' *as Christian preachers* in respect of *Christian preaching* to 'those in front of us'. We may be interested in philosophy, sociology, anthropology, music, art and the like, and such interests are far from irrelevant to our engagement with our contemporary culture, but such interests are not the *primary* lenses through which we approach the material.

Primarily we approach this material as preachers asking what it all means for preaching. This is our point of entry, our 'angle'. Such an 'angle' intersects the postmodern, post-Christian themes at a number of levels.

Engaging ideas

Sometimes, for example, we must engage with the *ideas* and *beliefs* presented in the material, and attempts at such engagement are included here. The philosophies, concepts and convictions of our contemporary culture challenge us (positively and negatively) and we must respond to the challenge.

Engaging contemporary people

But preaching is more than engaging with the ideas and beliefs of a culture. As has already become clear in earlier pages, preaching is essentially engaging *people* in a particular cultural context. 'Those in front of us' are crucially important to Christian preachers, and never more so than in a postmodern climate with its emphasis on contextualisation. Preaching is, after all, an essentially *personal* medium of communication in the sense that sermons are preached to people. The image of engaging with postmodern people, who possess various ideas and beliefs, rather than the ideas and beliefs for their own sake, is the method adopted here. The effect of this is that engagement with ideas and beliefs is undertaken with a human face in mind.

Application to preaching and preachers

This engagement with some of the ideas and characteristics of contemporary people leads inevitably to some attempts at *application*. First we are concerned to learn *what kind of preaching* is likely to communicate the Christian gospel best to people living in our postmodern, post-Christian culture. What does our engagement with contemporary people, their ideas and beliefs, likes and dislikes, presuppositions and assumptions, mean for the *content* and *style* of our preaching? Second is the related issue of learning *what kind of preacher* is best likely to communicate the gospel to such people. It is very important not to dismiss this practical input as mere 'technique', the poor relation of 'real' material dealing with philosophical ideas and intellectual concepts. Postmodernity sees no such distinction and regards such a view as a reductionist and inadequate understanding of both people and communication, a legacy of modernity. Indeed, we will discover that *the preacher* is very important in our postmodern, post-Christian context. But then, perhaps, that should not take us by surprise; Christianity has always been best represented and communicated incarnationally rather than 'philosophically'. Here, then, 'practical application' is presented alongside (and is sometimes interwoven with) material dealing with ideas and concepts. That may frustrate certain readers, but it's a postmodern way!

Some rules of engagement

A commitment to engage the ideas and people of a culture, from the perspective of the public proclamation of the Christian faith, is nothing new. To commit ourselves to such engagement is to become involved in the same kind of culture-friendly, counter-cultural, God-designed balancing act that Christian preachers have been undertaking since the first Christian Pentecost. Then, as now, the best engagement occurs when some ground rules are operating. The rules of engagement can be put like this. *Christian preachers must attempt to be as honest, open, gracious and challenging about both the gospel and the culture in which it is preached as they can be.* This compact statement needs unpacking, and in so doing engagement will begin quite naturally.

Honesty about the gospel . . .

We preachers cannot pretend to be what we aren't. We are people committed to the Christian faith and its public proclamation. Therefore, we are not engaging the ideas or people of contemporary culture with a pretend objectivity or neutrality and mustn't pretend we are. This is, like much else, a two-edged sword in respect of our contemporary culture. On the one hand we fall foul of the postmodern liking for permanent open-mindedness (provisionality) in the sense that we have nailed our colours to the Christian mast. On the other hand postmodernity dismisses 'objectivity' as a modernist illusion and is quite happy that everyone has an 'angle'. As we shall see, a great deal rides on *how* a person applies their 'angle', arrogance being abhorred but open authenticity being attractive.

Our prior commitment to the Christian faith has knock-on effects in terms of engagement. For example, our engagement with our cultural context, worthy though it is, is not regarded as an end in itself. The engaging of any culture with the gospel of Christ is an attempt to *change* that culture so that it increasingly resembles the kingdom of God. Cultures change – that very fact is the reason for this book being written. Cultures change when certain beliefs and values become natural and plausible to a significant number of people in a society. Those beliefs and values then begin to affect and shape that cultural context. Christian engagement with our own postmodern post-Christian culture has a clear aim, therefore; to identify ways and pursue means whereby Christian faith and discipleship can be perceived as a plausible and natural option for Western people.

Honesty about the gospel also means being open and taking risks. A person committed to engagement is open to being changed as much as seeking to effect change. When Paul stood before the Athenian philosophers, committed to the gospel as he was, there was the possibility that he could be 'talked out of it'. Risk is undertaken as an act of *faith*. Too often faith is understood in terms of security and non-risk whereas true faith is to trust God while engaging in risk-taking for the gospel. As Rudolph Bahro put it, 'When the forms of an old culture are dying the new culture is created by a few people who are not afraid to be insecure.'

Honesty about preaching . . . and preachers . . .

Many preachers reading chapter three will have got a clearer impression of what our contemporary culture *'makes of us'* than what we 'make of it'! The overall assessment appears to be 'not much' and some preachers may feel quite threatened by this. Our postmodern, post-Christian environment is at best dismissive and at worst hostile towards preaching. It is critical of preaching by both definition and implication. From a postmodern perspective Christian preaching is at best impossible and at worst immoral. It assumes the unassumable, that the meaning of language, the author's own intentions, the nature of the original context, is knowable and known, thus using language tyrannously. It presents the Christian faith as a metanarrative, a good news story applicable to all people in every time and place. It presents this 'big story' in terms of truth and ultimate reality, refusing the preferred way of provisionality and relativism. It is deemed to be inescapably authoritarian and paternalistic. These themes combined lead inevitably to preaching being regarded as manipulative and dehumanising. In short, from a radical postmodern, post-Christian perspective, preaching does not seem to have a great deal going for it.

Preachers, as the agents of this discredited activity, sometimes get caught up in the flak. Indeed, every time a preacher leads *public* worship (s)he declares what is no longer acceptable or tenable to very many secular, post-Christian people today – that the gospel of Jesus Christ is not merely private opinion. Whether or not we preachers actually fulfil this sorry stereotype is not the point. We may not feel guilty as charged, but common perceptions are highly significant and difficult to alter. Preachers used to be admired and respected, and perhaps in many churches still are. But in the broader cultural context, in terms of popularity stakes, preachers will be lucky to make 12th on a list of 13. Christian preachers have long lived with the charge that preaching is boring or irrelevant, the sharp end of postmodernity suggests something much more serious – preaching is undesirable. No wonder, then, that a leading dictionary now includes this definition of preaching: 'to give moral or religious advice in an obtrusive or tiresome way'. Dare we ever enter a pulpit again? Or dare we not?

So we need to remind ourselves, lest we have forgotten, that such antipathy towards the Christian gospel and those who proclaim it is nothing new. Peter and Paul certainly experienced it. The book of Acts and many occasions in Christian history record responses to preaching which make today's dismissiveness and 'hostility' look like a love affair. But we don't have to go so far back in time. Pre-postmodern preachers will remember how only several decades ago preachers were caricatured as out of touch buffoons prattling on about a transcendent God amidst a secular society committed to immanence and the death of God. Indeed, some suggest that the times when preaching and preachers do not make waves is really the time to worry. That we are coming to the end of a long era in which Christian faith was 'well connected' in terms of power and influence, that Christian influence in Western culture has been on the wane for a long time, is indisputable. Sad, perhaps, but we'll just have to get used to it. But let's not pretend that apathy and antipathy towards Christianity is new. It is merely re-emerging in a new cultural environment. Make no bones about it; preaching is an unpopular, counter-cultural activity and those who undertake it had better develop thick skins.

Yet, as we shall see, there is another side to this. Preachers who fulfil the stereotypes of boring, rational modernity and authoritarian, arrogant Christendom will become ever more unpopular. Preachers who reject these stereotypes need not. Preachers who relate to others not only as preachers but also as authentic people of Christian convictions, which they share sensitively, appropriately and with passion, will find our postmodern, post-Christian culture a challenging but by no means closed context in which to proclaim the Christian gospel.

Honesty about contemporary culture . . .

Some preachers, especially 'oldies' – that is, those who know they are non-native to the prevailing postmodern culture – will find it difficult to be honest and open in respect of 'what they make of it'. There may be barriers in the way of honest engagement; prejudices, pre-suppositions and prior preferences requiring to be identified then disarmed before honest engagement is possible. We look at a few possible 'barriers' to honest engagement with our contemporary culture.

- *A threatening enemy?*

The perception that the contemporary postmodern, post-Christian culture is a threatening enemy to Christian faith is a barrier to honest engagement for some preachers. Postmodernity is simply regarded as anti-Christian and its main themes a point-by-point denial of Christianity. Consequently there is considered to be no light in it at all and it is demonised. Evidence of antipathy, even hostility, towards Christianity is easily collected and feeds this perception. Just recently a young man exclaimed angrily to me when I acknowledged I was a Christian, 'Everything I like, you're against' (though quite how he knew this to be true I have no idea as we'd never met before). A negative response to such negativity is understandable. If contemporary culture dismisses Christianity and its advocates, why don't we just wipe the dust off our feet and have nothing to do with it? This jaundiced view, like all prejudices, is the result of making a universal application out of piecemeal evidence, and must be challenged on two counts.

First, it is simply not true that our contemporary cultural context is totally antipathetic towards Christianity. This culture, like many before it, is a mixed bag in relation to the Christian gospel and the Christian worldview. That is why engagement is never purely 'Pilgrim' or 'Indigenous' in nature and always more complicated than wholesale rejection or total acceptance of a prevailing culture. Certainly our contemporary culture asks serious questions of Christianity and its preachers, but it also provides many new opportunities, some of which will be identified later.

Second, even if the perception that contemporary culture is totally negative and hostile towards Christianity was wholly accurate, then could we really wipe the dust from our feet and opt out? If each time Jesus, his disciples, and those who came after them responded to rejection and apathy with rejection and apathy it is unlikely there would be anyone left today bearing the name 'Christian'. No one doubts that it is very difficult to be open and honest in a cultural context where you suspect what you believe and are is neither respected nor liked, but engagement becomes impossible if you respond by demonising that culture. Respective negative perceptions simply become more entrenched. So we must remember this: if God is not *already* at work in postmodern, post-Christian culture, then it will be a first! For the sake of the gospel, preachers today must seek gospel grace in their dealings with contemporary culture and its people. However difficult it may be, demonising it is not the way. Engagement is.

- *The challenge and cost of change*

The arrival of postmodernity and the continuing development of post-Christianity mean change, and change is nearly always threatening. As one wit put it, the only person who welcomes change is a baby with a dirty nappy! The only air Western Christianity has breathed for 200 years is that of modernity; small wonder then that many feel shivery as the cultural air-conditioning system changes. The challenge of cultural change for *preachers* is intense and represents for some a considerable barrier to honest engagement with our contemporary culture. The tension produced by the felt call of God to preach to those 'in front of you' while knowing that that requires honest engagement with new, potentially hostile themes is profound. Most preachers know that their preacher training was shaped by the principles of modernity and designed for the people of modernity. They now feel increasingly like blacksmiths noting the comparative numbers of horses and cars on the roads. Natives of pre-postmodernity, they know that to respond to God's continuing call and preach effectively in a postmodern context *entails retraining, relearning and reskilling*. This is a sharp challenge. To accept it is costly in many respects;

hence the temptation to reject the challenge to change but in so doing retain a barrier to honest engagement.

- *Removing rose-coloured spectacles*

A further and related barrier to honest engagement for some preachers is the reluctance to remove rose-coloured spectacles about the past. Faced with the challenges, changes and costs of our contemporary cultural context many preachers feel an understandable desire to wear rose-coloured specs, particularly in respect of their view of modernity and Christendom – the forerunners of postmodernity and post-Christianity. How lush and green the grass of modernity can suddenly appear compared to the bleak and barren postmodern landscape! How alien a post-Christian, secularised society can appear compared with the deferent respect of Christendom! Oh, bring back the old days!

However understandable such nostalgia may be, it begs to be seriously questioned. All too often the planks of modernity and Christendom are presented as the acceptable basis from which everything then went quickly downhill, and we must remind ourselves that 'modern thinking' and 'Christian thinking' were rarely the same thing, far from it, in fact. So an important step towards honest engagement with the emerging cultural context is a sober evaluation of the passing cultural context. Rose-coloured specs must be removed. Just what has modernist rationalism done for Christianity and in particular its preaching? Certainly, it brought about many enormous benefits to humanity in which Christian faith rejoices. But, in the words of Harry Poe, 'Modernity posed one of the greatest threats to Christianity that any culture has mounted.'[1] In terms of preaching it inculcated an aridity of thought and a wooden approach to interpretation. It defined the tools of the trade and decided that experts alone could use them adequately. It chose what should be illuminated and what shouldn't. It produced various forms of literalism while prohibiting valuable forms of imagination. It engendered a cerebral version of the Christian faith and fostered deism, agnosticism and atheism. Modernity may be familiar; we may have got used to living in it, even found our niche in it, but lush and green? Surely any grieving for its apparent passing is misplaced, even ironic? Or take Christendom. Another mixed blessing, some merits and demerits of which are sketched out in chapter two. Engagement with the emerging culture, then, must not be dogged by nostalgic, rosy views of the past that simply do not correspond to how things were.

• *Congregations today*

Some preachers may have to remove another pair of rose-coloured spectacles in order to engage honestly with contemporary culture. These they wear when they view their congregations whom they see in terms deeply influenced by centuries of Christendom. In a 'Christian culture' all congregations were pictured as devoutly *Christian.* A church service was a gathering of the faithful, eager to worship God, serve Christ, and listen to a preacher assert and declare a faith common and well-known to them all.

If such congregations ever existed (which is debatable), in our contemporary postmodern, post-Christian culture they almost certainly don't. Today's congregations are anything but generic and it is likely that every theme outlined in the previous chapter could be identified in congregations of any size. Congregations today rarely consist solely of fully paid-up believers but of those at various points along 'the way' in respect of Christian faith, including those 'just looking'. Some implications of preaching to such a diverse group of people will be identified at various points in the remaining chapters. It is sufficient here to note that the stereotypical, generic congregation for which some preachers continue to prepare sermons is less common than we think. To realise this, and be open to the implications of this, is to be better placed honestly to engage with our contemporary culture as Christian preachers.

To affect and infect our contemporary culture with the Christian gospel requires honest engagement with it. Such engagement is more likely to occur if Christian preachers refuse to demonise contemporary culture, are open to costly change, and remove rose-coloured spectacles in terms of how we regard the past and its imaginary congregations.

An important interlude . . . Hold on, there! A call to conversion reiterated

I can think of preachers who, on getting to about this point in the book, will be wondering if it has any relevance for them. They preach faithfully to small groups of faithful people, septuagenarians all, who together present a most generic-looking congregation. These congregations appear to be content with a preaching diet which flies in the face of much of what has been (and will be) said here. Preaching to 'those in front of us', such preachers might say, will mean continuing to preach just as we have done for decades.

I am not unsympathetic to that situation, indeed, I have preached regularly for several years in areas where sheep outnumber members of elderly congregations fifty-to-one, but I want to urge preachers tempted to opt out to hang on in there. The public and prophetic role of preaching means that 'those in front of us' must not become interpreted solely and always by the faithful few in the pew; Christian preaching has a wider remit than that. If we are honest, preachers know that there is sometimes pressure of various sorts, which combine to sustain the status quo, even when we know there is better way. I believe that *all* congregations will benefit from preaching that begins to take on board the insights arising from engaging in a postmodern context. Just because our faithful, small and aged congregations are not as critical about preaching as some, and have not left the church like many thousands of others have done, does not mean they will not welcome improvements. Indeed, I think many apparently 'contented' congregations are acutely aware that there is a widening gap between the 'church' area of their lives and other areas, and will welcome preaching that attempts to interpret and span the gap and reduce the sense of living in a ghetto.

In particular I consider that even with such small, settled congregations in mind, preaching is required to be evangelistic in the sense of sensitively and appropriately inviting people into a continuing living faith and offering resources for such discipleship. I believe the Christendom notion that settled churchgoers require 'teaching sermons' and only on those rare occasions when other folk turn up – and even rarer occasions when we move outside the church walls – is 'evangelistic preaching' required, is mistaken. Preachers should preach evangelistically to believers and non-believers alike, *for the benefit of all.* As William Willimon points out, many a baptised church member can live as a 'functional outsider', an amnesiac in terms of their faith. Preaching evangelistically to settled church congregations, therefore, enables 'forgetters' to become 'rememberers' for, as we come to realise increasingly, Christian conversion is a lifelong process.[2] Such preaching is also far more likely to communicate with postmodern seekers, sampling the Christian faith and the Christian Church. Preaching that relates how to find water in a desert is useful to everyone. Consequently much of what is advocated in what follows is not geared to a falsely distinguished context of believers and seekers but is appropriate and relevant to all. So, practising what I preach, I reiterate the 'call to commitment' outlined earlier and hope for continued engagement rather than disengagement.

5

POSITIVE ABOUT POSTMODERNITY?

What, then, do we make of postmodernity? In this chapter we begin with a broad assessment, then consider some of the more specific issues which were first raised in chapter three. Because the questions postmodernity poses about the nature of language constitute a central challenge to the preaching task those issues will be dealt with in a separate chapter.

Without falling into the trap of presenting an overly rosy sketch of the emerging *present* culture it must be said that many Christians find our contemporary cultural context highly stimulating, with much about it to welcome and affirm. Fundamentally, postmodernity has deemed modernity 'not enough', and many a Christian will concur with that judgement. Some see postmodernity as healing some of the sores of modernity while at the same time opening areas for plausible exploration that have long been taboo. Postmodernity puts spirituality – however understood – firmly back on the agenda of life. It reconnects thinking and feeling, seeing them as profoundly interwoven rather than unravelled. It is very much more open to the prophetic, mystical and intuitive dimensions of human existence, is much more 'right-hand brained'. It is better disposed to the idea of paradox, a category within which many of the central truths of Christianity fall. It is more relational and participative and communitarian than modernity. It places a high view on authenticity, especially authentic living, and is very critical of cheap and empty words. It is sensitive towards causes or groups that history has accorded a raw deal. It considers we have raped planet earth, subjugated women and privatised the soul and, therefore, displays openness to ecological, feminist/womanist and spiritual themes. What we currently call postmodernity isn't the finished article yet, of course (if such things are ever finished – like a jigsaw puzzle), and all assessments are, therefore, provisional, but as it looks at the moment it is not all bad news by any means. Indeed, in this pivotal, formative period, when certain searching questions once thought well taped down suddenly spring up again, Christianity has a wonderful opportunity to affect the postmodern mind with the gospel of Christ.

The significant preacher

This brief outline of some 'positive' postmodern themes demonstrates the potential significance of the *preacher* in preaching in our contemporary cultural context, a theme hinted at earlier and revisited more fully at this point. Postmodernity may dislike certainties and reject absolutes and dismiss dogmas but it places a high value on authenticity, relationality and personality. Consequently what the preacher appears to be *like*, *who* they are known to be and *how* a sermon is preached is as important as *what* is preached in terms of communicating the gospel to the people of this present age.

The preacher's personality, demeanour, integrity and the like have been repeatedly identified as aiding the cause of effective preaching for many years. We have long appreciated the fact that there is more to effective preaching in any cultural setting than simply the standard of the sermon. What is new in our contemporary cultural context is the *degree* to which such factors are significant. In the past the importance of the preacher in preaching has been cast mostly in functional and aesthetic terms – can she be heard, is that mannerism annoying, should he smile more often? These things were important mainly because they impeded the effectiveness of what was *said*, and, in the modernist way of things, what was *said* was regarded as primary. What was said *was* the sermon, everything else – method, technique, and communication skills – were aids. Without suggesting for a moment that *what* is preached is unimportant, it needs to be made clear that nowadays 'the sermon' is the words *and* 'everything else'. What has previously been thought of as the icing on the cake has become an iced cake! The medium is ever more closely tied up with the message. The preacher him/herself is more profoundly associated with the message they preach than ever before. A hundred and fifty years or so ago Phillips Brooks famously defined preaching as 'truth mediated through personality'. In terms of preaching in our contemporary cultural context, never has the 'personality' bit been more important. Any discussion of preaching in our postmodern, post-Christian context must, therefore, include the significance of the *who* and the *how* as well as the *what*. It is important this is borne in mind as we engage with some more specific postmodern and post-Christian themes.

A certain kind of certainty

The postmodern dislike of certainty poses certain problems. Many Christian preachers were trained with the mantra 'preach certainties, not doubts' ringing in their ears. To be certain is regarded by many as a key requirement of a preacher and some Christians equate good preaching with the degree of certitude with which preachers proclaim the Faith. Is this postmodern antipathy towards certainty one of those things to which Christians must respond 'Tough, that's the way it is'? I believe we can do better than that.

Faith and certainty

It is important to ask just what kind of certainty we are called to proclaim and what kind of certainty postmodern culture dislikes so much. Are we talking about the same thing? A sure and certain *faith* in God through Christ is not the same as stark certainty. We are, after all, Christian *believers* and our certainties arise out of our faith. The fruit of faith is faithfulness, which is at its most attractive when quietly confident rather than arrogantly aggressive. So 'certain', meaning 'I believe this to be true', has more going for it than 'certain' meaning 'I am right.'

The certainty of modernity

Perhaps the problem is as acute as it is because so much of our 'certainty talk' was forged in the heat of our engagement with modernity, and sounds like it. Then, in order to get a hearing, you had to evince certainty. You argued for Christianity on the grounds that it could be 'proved' and, as the outcome of such proof one could be 'certain' – like a scientist is certain of the results of an oft-repeated experiment. It is somewhat ironic that preachers should find that a strong plus of preaching in the context of high modernity is becoming a weak minus in the emerging culture of postmodernity. Just as postmodernity parts company with the fixed, definite certainties of modernity so it finds preaching that is wedded to its moods and methods particularly distasteful.

So much of our Christian faith has come to be understood and subsequently presented in terms of fixed certainties and 'definitive' statements. The Ten Commandments are not now best known for their flexibility (nor, in my experience, are those preachers who regularly use them as texts!) but originally, as God's rules for life, they possessed an enormous capacity for liberty and flexibility. Christian Creeds are not generally thought of as fluid statements, but rather as material that has been 'sorted'. Yet the possible interpretations able to be properly identified in and applied from the Creeds are wonderful to explore. The ways of modernity have also affected our presentation of 'doctrines'. Rarely are they presented as what they are – the fruit of faithful Christians reflecting on and engaging with their own faith and cultural context. Too often they are presented like *Blue Peter* recipes – 'And here is one the Church made earlier. Follow the instructions carefully, yours should look the same as this.'

Readers must not hear what I am not saying. I am not arguing that preachers cease to use the Commandments, Creeds or doctrines of our Faith. I am contending for the view that our current understanding and application of our Christian faith so often bears the marks of engagement with modernity and, therefore, exudes a 'got it sussed' quality that postmodern people find very unattractive. Rather than reject this core Christian material, preachers need to begin to learn how to preach it in a different cultural context and one characterised by a widespread ignorance of basic Christianity. Such a context emphasises the need for being inventive with communicating the message while not being complicated with the message itself. Preachers are required to be both story-keepers and storytellers. I am not talking about dumbing-down the gospel, but clarity regarding the heart of Christian faith. Given the deeply human contexts which produced the Commandments, the profound mysteries enshrined in the Creeds and the wonderful richness of our doctrines (not to mention the magnificent Sermon on the Mount!), the call to replace fixed certainties of arrogance with living certainties of faith could be a wake-up call from God!

The arrogance of Christendom

If modernity produced a certain kind of certainty, Christendom produced the arrogant air with which such certainty was proclaimed. After hundreds of years of expecting to be listened to and demanding to be heard, it comes as a bit of a shock to realise that 'an authoritative air' is a definite turn-off for increasing numbers of 'those in front of us'. A recurrent theme in both postmodernity and post-Christianity is disenchantment with authorities and a deep dislike of élites – a 'flight from deference' as one writer puts it. There is little doubt that Western Christianity's long association and identification with power and authority is increasingly haunting it today. Like it or not preachers are closely identified not so much with a life-giving gospel as a life-restricting, corrupt institution. They are seen as the representatives of Christianity, just as I did to the young man who 'liked everything I didn't', and what preachers represent often speaks louder than what they say. The natural disposition of many people today towards preaching is, therefore, resistant. The more authoritatively we claim to speak the less effective we are likely to be. Few preachers *intend* their preaching to be perceived like this, but for many people that is just how it is perceived.

Authentic faithfulness

How are preachers to respond to this? Well, simply to be aware of it is a step in the right direction. One deliberate response is regularly to check the 'atmosphere' – the air – of the *content* of our sermons and also the way we *deliver* them. So often our sermons present us as 'in charge'. It is 'us who know, telling you who don't'. 'We' have 'got it' and 'they' haven't. So often all our stories and illustrations come from a position of dominance or power or wisdom. That simply will not do in this contemporary context, nor can we really be happy with such a situation from the point of view of the gospel. We know we are servants of the Servant, let's declare *that* more regularly. We know we have not 'got it all sussed' at all, but that we live by faith and trust in Christ. Let's be more 'up front' about doubt, not in the modernist sense of provocative 'I do not really believe in the virgin birth . . .' type sermons but in the sense that we are people whose searching and doubts *have* been met and *are* being met by God in Jesus Christ. After all, the antithesis of faith is faithlessness, not doubt. The honest doubt of a searching heart is common to us all, and for many of us was the beginning of faith.

Postmodern preaching, therefore, will tend to be personal rather than abstract. It will be a sharing of self, as a person of faith, rather than merely a sharing of ideas or doctrines. The era of cool professional 'distance' between preacher and people has gone, indeed it is now a liability. The wrong signals are sent out by keeping our own weaknesses and struggles permanently out of the pulpit, not that they are flaunted or used manipulatively, but that they are part of who we are, and who we are as Christian people rather than simply as preachers is now very significant. Colin Morris tells a lovely story of a train announcer. With her most official voice she announced to a crowded platform of those heading to work the lateness of train after train. Nobody batted an eyelid, it was par for the course. The tannoy speaker crackled for the umpteenth time and the standard announcement began 'We regret to announce the delay of . . .' Then there was a pause, a big sigh, and she continued, 'You have no idea how embarrassing I find all this, I'm really sorry everyone, honest . . .' The folk on the crowded platform froze and then turned and faced the loudspeakers. The announcer had given up informing and had begun communicating. So let's be more honest and human rather than sustaining the 'holy ones six feet above contradiction' image which rather than generating respect now produces incredulity. Why should we need to pretend that we are what we are not? Especially when 'we' as believers, and our honesty and authenticity are very important in the business of communicating the gospel to contemporary people. Authentic faithfulness is a more persuasive sermon than arrogant certainty – probably because it's more Christian.

Vive la différence?/Relatively speaking

'Vive la différence!' (note how '!' has now become '?') and 'Relatively speaking' in chapter three outlined three themes in particular which we reflect on here. What do we make of the closely-related issues of *pluralism, relativism* and *metanarratives*, or 'big stories'?

Concerning pluralism

The postmodern assumption that a plurality of views or beliefs is always better than any single view or belief, and that no single view or belief can be judged to be better or more valid than any other as they are relative, begs to be challenged. Surely some things are perceived to be better than others, otherwise why do more people want a Mercedes than a Lada, or prefer Häagen-Dazs ice-cream to the local supermarket 'saver' brand? Surely love is better than hate, peace better than war, trying to do good better than deliberately doing evil? Preachers are those who proclaim that the gospel of Jesus Christ *is* good news. They propose Christianity, not impose it. They announce that God's sober judgement about human beings is not the end point of the story but a new starting point for human freedom, identity and renewal. They affirm that to choose Christ and enter the Christian way is a good choice to make and a good way to take. They declare that anyone can taste and see (and seek to find ways to enable postmodern people to do so?). From this work, Christian preachers must not cease.

What will probably need to cease, however, are knee-jerk negative reactions to pluralism. We can do better than that. Although pluralism of the kind we currently experience in the West is a relatively recent phenomenon and a pretty virulent form, Christianity has existed in cultural contexts of pluralism since its inception. The context in which the early Christians preached and Christianity grew was one of great religious and cultural pluralism. Some very ancient Christian Churches have never lived in any other context. Indeed, Christians living in a Christendom context when, ostensibly, everyone is deemed to be Christian, creating a 'Christian culture', is the main exception to the rule. More Christians than not have lived out their faith in a pluralist context.

A look at the world Church today leads to the conclusion that Christianity seems to be a good deal healthier in situations of religious and cultural plurality than in situations where we continue the pretence of being 'Christian cultures'. Nor do these Christian Churches seem to be rejecting or surrendering central themes of Christian faith in order to accommodate the beliefs and feelings of others. On the contrary a context of plurality often seems to sharpen up faith no end. Lesslie Newbigin encapsulates the stance of many Christians living long-term in a context of religious and cultural pluralism when he states, 'We cannot set limits on the grace of God but we do know no other Saviour.'[1] It seems, therefore, that only those who take for granted the dominance and authority of Christendom look askance at contemporary Western pluralism; everyone else views it as business as usual. The indisputable existence of pluralism in our own contemporary context is, whatever else it is, a sure sign that Christendom Christianity is nearing its sell-by date, if not already past it. Wilbert Shenk rightly refers to the 'lengthening shadows of Christendom'. We must see pluralism for what it is, not the spectre it isn't. The significant presence of pluralism among us does not mean that Christianity has no place or role or voice, it simply means that its place and role and voice are worked out among others. Western pluralism potentially frees Christianity from a form of cultural domination that is not only deeply unattractive to postmodern people but which has nullified and deadened it for as long as anyone can remember. Stripped of cultural dominance, no longer possessing any means of compulsion, Western Christianity can offer contemporary culture nothing other than Christ. What's so bad about that?

Concerning relativism

Relativism presents a serious challenge to Christian faith and it is significant that while many Christians around the world accept their pluralist context they *reject* the assumptions of relativism. The idea that Christianity is one option among many is self-evident in a pluralist context, but the notion that Christian Faith *merely consists of relative ideas and concepts* and that its only truth and reality lies with those who choose to believe it, is rejected as something quite different. It is hardly surprising that this distinction is made. The assertion that there *cannot* be ultimate truth or reality flies in the face of Christian faith. Christian preachers, of many theological shades and hues, will want to assert the ultimate reality of God: Father, Son and Holy Spirit. Very many Christians, including this author, will want to affirm the truth of Jesus Christ with a capital 'T', and assert that the 'scandal of particularity' is not God's accident as much as God's design. In this sense Christian preachers will reject the postmodern assumption about the rightness of relativism and this will be reflected in their preaching.

But we can make a better response to relativism than simple rejection and this, too, needs reflecting in our preaching. In our continuing commitment to ultimate reality and truth in Christian terms we must make sure we are not tying one hand behind our backs. We do that if we fail to recognise that alongside a deep commitment to relativism, perhaps even *because* of it, postmodernity provides a context for a more holistic understanding of reality and truth than modernity permitted to be presented. Postmodernity provides preachers with new opportunities to present the gospel as 'real' and 'true'.

It is really a question of accepting how we come to *know* things (technically known as epistemology). Modernity, for example, stressed a particular method of knowing things by which it allowed things to be declared 'true' or 'real'. Only when this method was followed could something be said to be true. Not surprisingly, therefore, the truth claims of the Christian gospel followed this method; preachers applied modernist epistemology to the proclamation of Christian faith, and with some success. When Christian thought had passed through the fires of modernist epistemology it was deemed 'objectively' real and true; reality and truth that had, according to Christians, passed the test set by modernity. It is in this sense that the radical relativism of postmodernity challenges Christian views of truth and reality, because those views were forged in a cultural context that is now being increasingly rejected and we feel we have much to lose. Maybe we have. But I want to advance the view that just as we must not put our legs in the air and play dead concerning God's truth in Christ neither must we be bamboozled into thinking that our presentation of God's truth in Christ must conform to criteria set by modernity.

Postmodernity accepts more ways of knowing what we know than modernity did, and, therefore, employs a more varied epistemology. It helpfully reminds us that much that we know and often value most does not, can not and ought not to conform to modernist ways of knowing. It is far more sympathetic to the view that *how* we come to know things must be appropriate to the type of knowledge with which we are dealing. So modernist epistemology may well be OK for certain kinds of experiments but does not work well when applied to love or faith. If we went to a dentist who informed us that she knew how to remove our teeth because she'd read it up the night before in a book of poetry, we'd be out of her surgery like a shot if we had any sense. The boy telling his girl that he loves her on the basis of proof supplied by his latest laboratory experiment indicates the problem the other way round. Consequently, though they may well accord them no *ultimate* reality, postmodern people are open to the truth and reality of love, loyalty, mystery and relationships. Indeed, if people encounter these things in Christian friends and congregations the preacher is provided with a powerful primer from which to invite such people into a faith experience of the ultimate reality of God and the Truth of Jesus Christ.

Philosophically the postmodern commitment to relativism remains a problem, but the very commitment to relativism opens new avenues of presenting truth and reality which Christian preachers will do well to employ. A wide epistemology should characterise contemporary sermons. Meaningful ways of interpreting Christian truth claims must be found. 'Telling stories', a phrase often related to lies, can be an effective way of proclaiming truth. Risks must be taken. George Hunter has suggested that preaching must correspond to the ways in which people appear to *experience* the Christian faith rather than 'classical theology'. For example, beginning with Jesus' humanity rather than his divinity at least emulates the faith journey of his first disciples. Tradition presents the Holy Trinity as 'Father, Son and Holy Spirit', but today and in the New Testament, this is not the most common order of people's experience of the Christian Godhead. Evangelical received wisdom always has repentance preceding any sort of faith commitment, but contemporary people sample and shop and as a result a sense of commitment often precedes any awareness of repentance.

Concerning metanarratives

What are we to make of the postmodern rejection of metanarratives, the 'big stories' of human existence? Probably our first response is to acknowledge joyously and humbly that our Christian faith is indeed what postmodernity defines as a metanarrative. We cannot, we would not want to do away with the notion that Christianity is a 'big story', a story so deeply rooted in God's overarching, gracious saving purposes for all creation that our only option is to plead guilty as charged. Any attempt to dismantle our metanarrative and pretend that nothing is lost by splitting up the story into a multitude of free-standing unconnected micronarratives is a serious mistake as the sum of the parts is probably greater than the parts themselves. Our story is the gospel (in the broadest sense) and we are defined by it. It is, echoing the words of Andrew Walker, the story that tells us who we are, where we come from and where we are going. It is the story which has given meaning and hope to millions of ordinary folk, down through history and all around the globe. We are left, therefore, with the prospect, however difficult, of remaining committed to our big story in a cultural context that is, by definition, incredulous towards it. How might we defend such a position?

- *Many metanarratives*

We might want repeatedly to draw attention to certain things. First, that Christianity is not alone in retaining a commitment to an 'overarching story'. In his little book, *Into The 21ˢᵗ Century*, Donald English pointed out that just as some elements of contemporary culture appear endlessly to fragment and rule out big stories, others do not. He noted how often 'comprehensive pictures of humanity' appear in certain fields of knowledge, in some schools of genetics, for example, and how – relevant to our later discussion on the relativity of language – some linguists are positing the idea that all languages may in fact derive from one basic source.[2] Postmodernity may retain its incredulity towards metanarratives but it appears that, at least for the foreseeable future, there will remain various 'big stories' to remain incredulous about.

- *The importance of metanarratives*

Second, Christians, not least Christian preachers, may want to contend, as Reynolds Price does, for the importance of metanarratives. Price argues that 'big stories' that declare who and what we are, are for human beings second in importance only to sources of physical nourishment.[3] Therefore, to abandon metanarratives is like smoking: it seriously damages human health. To sustain our commitment to the Christian metanarrative, then, while remaining alert and sensitive to its perceived drawbacks, might well become a long-term service to humankind.

- *Postmodern metanarratives?*

Third, we can draw attention to the fact that postmodernity itself might be said to be developing its own 'big stories'. In other words some metanarratives appear more incredulous to the postmodern mind and spirit than others. Postmodernity is not yet what it will become, it is under construction. Inevitably when things are under construction there is a lot of demolishing before new building takes place, and we may well discover that 'incredulity towards metanarratives' relates more to the process of demolition than rebuilding. We should also note (though it comes from a different 'compartment' in life and we must remember that postmodernity requires no coherence between 'compartments') that the rejection of 'everything being found in one place' is itself sometimes rejected. Take, for example, the huge shopping malls springing up outside increasing numbers of cities. The next generation on from the supermarket (the continuing success of which lies in everything being found in one place!) shopping malls give the impression of variety, choice, difference. But is self-deception going on? Not only are all the respective retail outlets virtually identical in every mall but the whole point of the mall is that despite being made up of 200 shops everything *is* in the same place. Whether malls represent commercial micronarratives or disguised commercial metanarratives is open to discussion, as is the long-term postmodern rejection of each and every metanarrative.

Presenting the story

Fourth, while remaining committed to our Christian metanarrative *its very nature* demands that it is presented in the most helpful way possible for people – even highly sceptical postmodern post-Christian people – to encounter and accept it. In other words, though the Christian gospel *is* a metanarrative, does it always have to be presented in such a way as to instantly appear one? I would argue not. We might note that few – if any – of those who encountered Jesus were presented with the 'big picture'. The rich young ruler is told to give away his wealth and follow, the woman at the well to bring her husband, Nicodemus to be 'born again'. Jesus nearly always adopts a very apt, personal application of good news to those he encounters. Of course, he could declare the Grand Design, and did, but almost always to those who were already his disciples, those who were 'with him'. Significantly, however, it has to be said it was the 'big picture' that his disciples failed to grasp time and again, especially prior to his resurrection. Put simply, presenting the 'big picture' is rarely the best starting place, especially for the hotchpotch of folk that make up today's congregations. In this respect postmodern, post-Christendom people are very much like pre-modern, pre-Christendom people. Nowadays an awareness of the 'big story' comes later, when a person explores what is happening to them and begins to make some sense of it. Rarely do contemporary people who become Christian respond initially to 'the big picture', the Christian metanarrative. They, like those who encountered Jesus in the gospels, respond better to the apt application of good news to their own situation. It would appear, therefore, that Christianity is best *experienced* as a metanarrative rather than initially presented as one. Seekers *discover* the gospel to be their overarching story rather than being informed that it is one.

Applying insights . . .

This clearly has implications for our preaching. How contemporary people find their way into the metanarrative called Christianity is of vital importance to preachers so we spend some time flying a few kites.

- *From micro to meta – the way in?*

Our preaching will more likely be effective communication when we go from the micronarrative to the (connected) metanarrative, from the little story to the big story, from the local to the universal, rather than vice versa. Stephen Toulmin makes much the same point from the other direction when he comments that postmodernity marks the shift from the written to the oral, from the universal to the particular, from the general to the local, and from the timeless to the timely.[4] In the lovely phrase of Andrew Walker we begin with 'the one short tale we feel to be true'[5] and let it work its magic. This may mean that we consciously tell the kind of micronarratives that are effective catalysts for producing openness to the metanarrative. Rick Warren suggests that 'topical exposition' is more effective than 'verse to verse exposition' in communicating to contemporary people. Rather than a text leading to a theme, a life-theme is worked out in relation to the Christian 'big story'. Walter Brueggemann talks about 'funding the postmodern imagination' by which he means that Christianity offers lots of little pieces out of which people can put life together in fresh configurations. Donald English, especially in the years immediately prior to his untimely death, repeatedly reminded preachers that their job was so to present the gospel *and* human life that people said, 'There is more to this than I thought.' The postmodern acceptance of several ways of coming to 'know' things gives new scope for imaginative Christian preaching.

- *Considering context*

We will need to pay as much attention to the *contexts* in which we preach as we do the *texts* from which we preach. If this sounds obvious it is worth noting that Mark Greene[6] has noted how the British preaching tradition has tended to focus upon generic rather than audience-oriented methods of preaching. Compared with some American homileticians who have placed great stress on listening, British homiletical methods have paid much less attention to the diverse nature of the hearers. Greene uses worthies such as Martin Lloyd-Jones and John Stott, whose books on preaching (*Preaching and Preachers* and *I Believe In Preaching*, respectively) are on more preachers' bookshelves than most, to illustrate this point. Lloyd-Jones views all hearers as patients suffering from the same disease. It is called sin and he writes how 'it is a vital part of preaching to reduce all listeners to that common denominator'. Stott pays more attention to context and congregation but, claims Greene, who picks up Stott's own analogy of playing chess, always wants to 'play white'. That is, he appears to be much more concerned how people respond to the preacher rather than how the preacher responds to the people. Whether or not Greene is right about these British 'worthies', we note that such a generic, 'deaf' approach to preaching is increasingly ineffective in our contemporary cultural context. The 'herald' who knows the message and simply delivers it to whoever – like the sandwich-board preacher outside the Christian bookshop – cannot be said to be completely redundant; after all, the gospel is good news to everyone. Nevertheless, those who are *also* 'inquirers', who pay attention to who is out there and respond appropriately are likely to be the more effective preachers today. Shoemaker's *Outside the Door* strikes this balance: 'Near enough to God to hear him, and know he is there, but not so far from people as to not hear them.' Listening and responding is a better way for preachers today, just as it was for apostolic preachers.

Paying much more attention to context begs questions of some contemporary models of preaching. To pay attention to 'context', especially local contexts, requires both *knowledge* (knowledge of the locality, its communities, the local issues that are 'hot potatoes', the nature of the church community etc) and the *skills* required to relate such knowledge to the gospel and vice versa. This not only requires knowledge but also being *known*, having a relationship with 'those in front of us'. It is hard to see how the 'local itinerancy' system of some denominations, where a preacher preaches in umpteen places once in a blue moon, can produce sufficient attention to context or enable the preacher to become 'known', so that their preaching promises to cut most ice in our contemporary cultural climate. On the other hand, if a preacher is truly 'local' (not simply in terms of geography but also in terms of cultural and social *identity*), then the possibilities of effective, authentic preaching taking place increase enormously. And if a preacher is *known* and *respected* locally not simply as a *preacher* – but also as parent, local teacher or mechanic or swimming pool attendant or whatever – the potential effectiveness of their preaching in relation to the folk that make up contemporary congregations increases yet again. It is worth noting, therefore, that lay/local preaching is potentially disastrous or potential dynamite in respect of our contemporary culture. If the Churches use lay preachers poorly, employing systems that engender hit-and-run generic preaching for faceless, generic, imaginary congregations, they will assist the continuing numerical decline of practising Christians in the West. But if Churches use them sensitively, enabling a true 'localness' and encouraging them to adopt the best forms of incarnational ministry they, more than full-time clergy, could become the most effective formal communicators of the gospel the Church currently possesses. There is a need, therefore, to look long and hard at how 'local' preaching operates and an equal need to encourage and permit a much wider social and cultural group of people to become local preachers than is often the case. The charge levied at magistrates, that they were middle-aged, middle-of-the-road – middle-everything with a 'blue rinse' – must not be true of today's Christian preachers.

- *Preaching in context – the wider pastoral context of the local church*

How people discover and experience and respond to Christianity also clearly sets the *preaching activity itself* in a wider context. It is my belief that sensitive, culturally-attuned Christian preaching remains valid today and is vital. It is indisputable, however, that preaching is most effective when it is part of a wider package of experiences and belonging that fall mainly within the life and ministry of the local church. As Lesslie Newbigin has stated, 'The only possible hermeneutic of the gospel is a congregation which believes it.'[7] Churches that do not help people make sense of their lives and find purpose and meaning through their friendships and activities, in their meetings and homes, will find their pulpit a pretty sterile place, even if it produces great erudition and rhetoric. Local churches whose whole life consists of Sunday worship find, paradoxically, that preaching is weakened, not strengthened, by this focus.

Preaching which emerges out of *shared experiences* is more potent and effective than that which begins with the application of dogma. Ministers know that, and often rightly feel that their most effective preaching goes on before a couple, a coffin or a font, particularly when it follows honest pastoral conversations. For lay and ordained preachers alike in a very real sense their sermon has begun before ever they get in the pulpit and doesn't end when they leave it. How often congregations invite a 'special preacher' to a special occasion only to think afterwards, we prefer our normal preacher!

- *Preaching in context – the wider liturgical context of public worship*

There is another context that must be mentioned here and it concerns the role and understanding of preaching in the wider liturgical context of an act of public worship. Getting this right is crucial as we face the immediate future. The most effective preaching in our contemporary cultural setting will include the creative and imaginative use of *every* aspect of public worship (including imaginative uses we haven't thought of yet!). I contend that worship needs to proclaim 'our Story' with more flair, colour, movement, corporate involvement and participation, and the use of all five senses. Our services need to exude an authentic quality of the faith family being themselves as they offer worship to God.

Postmodern people, with their openness to spirituality and mystery, will particularly benefit from an overall experience of worship that enables them to *worship* and the sermon is at its best when part of such public worship. The effective sermon today cannot be disengaged from other elements of worship, if ever it could. Effective preaching in a postmodern context, therefore, challenges some aspects of *old and new practices alike* concerning the role of preaching in worship.

The old Free Church practice of leaving the sermon until last is not a good model for public worship. There are increasing numbers of contemporary people for whom a repetitive pedestrian procession of worship elements leading to the primacy of the pulpit simply doesn't work. It all too often produces a wooden, cerebral feel to the service and inhibits the possibility that the worship will 'reach' people. Moreover, this pattern of worship does not give sufficient time or space for creative and imaginative *response* to preaching (and thereby sends the signal that no response is necessary or at the very least is insignificant). Singing a hymn and going home just will not do. Indeed, if moved, increasing numbers of contemporary people want to *do* something, to mark, express, embody in some way what they feel. The ambience of worship of which the sermon is part and in which the sermon is set is crucial, and each and every suggestion of how preaching in our contemporary context might be more effective must include taking very seriously the implications for the whole act of public worship. Consequently preachers must work as hard on this wider worship context as on the sermon itself. For many people today the sum of worship is greater than the parts.

The growing trend of local worship leaders, greater participation, varied music and the like has much to commend it in terms of its postmodern friendliness. There are, however, dangers becoming evident, the main one being the separation of preaching from all other elements of worship. The tendency in more and more churches is to have a 'time of worship', then invite the preacher to preach, then 'have some more worship'. If challenged about this I am sure most if not all would affirm that preaching *was* part of the worship, but increasingly common tendencies in language and practice signal otherwise. Just as the 'all things lead to the sermon' model of worship is not the most effective in our contemporary context, nor is a model which suggests preaching is merely an insert to the essential business of singing! In this context too, therefore, preachers and all those involved in worship planning and preparation must work hard on *every* aspect and the integration of the whole. In both contexts – old and new – preaching today needs to be set more fully and holistically in the context of public worship. Here, as on a number of occasions, this applies to *both* those long in the tooth when it comes to church attendance and Christian believing and those who are just dipping their toes in the water. Good preaching set in good worship is beneficial to everyone.

Incarnational preaching

We have already noted that *authenticity* is more persuasive than *authority* in our contemporary culture, and much more valued by its people, and also noted some ramifications for our preaching. It means the instruction many of us received when we were training – 'leave yourself out of your sermons' – has now had its day. Now we must put 'ourselves' in them. Not, it must be made clear, so that sermons become a never-ending stream of personal anecdotes (we've all met those preachers!), or so that personality obliterates the gospel, but rather that the preacher represents a personality *formed* by the gospel. Consequently a preacher's own gospel story is significant, and that they believe and live it is as significant as that they can rationally explain it. What we are really noting is the significance of the *relationship* between preacher and hearer which gives rise to *incarnational* preaching. Sermons are more than the words that make them up. Perhaps it has always been so. Jesus Christ was The Word . . . and he became flesh and lived among us. Perhaps Christian preachers themselves are incarnational micronarratives enabling some contemporary people to enter into an experience of the Christian metanarrative?

Perhaps these responses combined are our best 'not guilty' plea to the charge that our metanarrative is, by definition, inherently corrupting and dominating. People who have encountered sensitivity rather than dominance and experienced freedom rather than incarceration are a powerful witness in this respect.

6

WELL, WHAT *ARE* WORDS WORTH?

W hat do we make of the postmodern claim that words and language are relative, that they possess no 'real' significance but are simply self-referential? At one level this notion is an easy target for ridicule. Speaking at a conference, Alister McGrath noted wryly that linguistic relativists apply the principle of relativity to all words except those making up their own contract of employment. Suddenly, when dealing with salaries and conditions, words mean exactly what they say!

Yet the postmodern assumption about the relativity of language presents a profound challenge to Christian preachers, especially in terms of how we understand, use and apply our most indispensable resource, *the Bible*. After all, preachers are those who, in a variety of ways, affirm the Christian scriptures as 'the word of God' and it doesn't require a genius to work out that the relativity of all language poses serious questions to such a view. I am aware, however, that whole rain forests are disappearing in order to produce material on issues that here must be flagged up in just a few paragraphs, and so plead guilty to the charge of superficiality and having a bias towards identifying some practical implications for preaching and preachers.

Relativism rejected

The view that all words and language are relative is in fact challenged and rejected by every act of Christian preaching. An acceptance that the biblical text is completely relative ultimately leaves the preacher with nothing to preach. In effect postmodernity denies the possibility that divine revelation can be mediated through an inspired text, and although preachers will have different ideas about what 'revelation' and 'inspired' may mean, few will feel able to live with the ramifications of this particular piece of postmodern thinking. Instead, Christian preaching proceeds on the basis that God's nature and intentions *can* be discerned in and through biblical texts. Christian preachers assume that the Holy Spirit of God illuminates the minds of the Christian community, of which the preacher is a part, so that the meanings of scripture can be rightly discerned. They trust that God's Spirit has been about this business since the beginnings of Christianity and, therefore, what has been discerned by Christians over the centuries, forming the Christian Tradition, remains relevant. They believe that the God of the Bible not only acts but also *speaks* and that what is *said* can be rightly discerned and apprehended. They suspect that the Fourth Gospel presentation of Christ as the divine *Word*, rather than the divine anything else, is highly significant. They realise that to obey the 'Great Commission', going into all the world teaching everything Jesus has commanded, is strictly impossible if radical relativity rules. They realise that the gospel must be proclaimed afresh to every changing context, but believe it can be while remaining identifiably Christian. Christian preaching, then, by definition, in both theory and practice, rejects radical linguistic relativity.

Bye-bye historical criticism?

The assumption that all language is relative stands in sharp contrast to the principles that produced the historical critical methods by which almost all preachers reading this book will have been trained, and it is in this respect that many preachers will feel the sting of linguistic relativity most acutely. Put simply, historical critical methodology is regarded as a product of modernity and is thereby subject to postmodern criticism and rejection. Postmodernity considers the aims and intentions of historical criticism as illusory and misguided. In relation to the Bible, historical critical methods sought 'original' material: the original intention of a biblical author, the original context in which a text was produced, the original meaning of the original words. Postmodern biblical interpretation deems such material beyond knowing and, therefore, declares the search pointless. As we can't recreate the author or the text, why try? The impossibility of knowing what a text meant to the original reader(s) means that what the text means now, to the present reader(s), becomes highly significant; indeed, it is claimed to be all we have. Biblical texts, therefore, can only be applied relatively rather than objectively or absolutely. Among other things, this has given rise to an explosion of 'perspectives' by which biblical material is interpreted and preachers will have noticed how any decent book on biblical interpretation nowadays contains feminist/ womanist, post-patriarchal, political, black, urban, poststructuralist and reader-response approaches to scripture, and probably many more. It is already being noted, however, that while such 'perspectivism' appears very postmodern-friendly, the tendency to 'hijack' the meaning of scripture by seeing it through a particular lens is yet another example of the authoritarian and totalising tendency so deeply despised by postmodernity.

So the jury is out on the continuing worth of historical critical methodology and the main insights it has produced. Some writers suggest it is dead in the water while others believe it continues to have value and usefulness. This debate, beginning rather than ending, is already filling huge tomes and cannot be taken on board here. The aim here is simply to identify some of the implications for preaching. As a preacher I tend to the view that historical critical methodology must be neither totally rejected nor wholly accepted but instead re-evaluated in the light of our emerging postmodern context. Today many folk are cagey about the claims of historical critical methodologies, but being cagey is quite different to outright rejection. We may be less certain that X meant Y but does that mean that every X means nothing at all? The claim that we can't know anything for sure is as absolute as the claim that we can know everything. Is the only choice to swallow everything or spit it all out? Over the last two centuries the dominance of historical-critical methods has undoubtedly brought immense benefits and rewards, not least our growing appreciation of the historical and cultural aspects of scripture. These methods have produced valuable insights that are the stock in trade of many a good preacher. So we must take care not to throw out any babies with the bath water while realising that the bath water needs changing, or at the very least hotting up a little.

Wither expository preaching?

Nowhere is the postmodern challenge to historical critical methodology felt more acutely than in respect of 'expository' preaching with its emphasis on uncovering and exposing the meaning of a biblical text. Perhaps no surprise, then, that some renowned expository preachers assert that historical critical methods and insights must continue to fuel preaching in a postmodern context, and seek to counter some of the main charges levied against expository preaching.[1]

The charge that expository preaching is rationalistic elicits a sharp counter-attack from its proponents. Our current disenchantment with rationalism must not lead us to reject the gains of the scientific revolution and embrace medieval myth and magic. Postmodernity has not yet carried the day for everyone and exposition remains a valuable tool in reaching the many 'secular people' who remain critical realists rather than postmodern relativists. It was, after all, the biblical worldview that gave birth to the scientific method. Also, given that many of the views currently associated with postmodernity are so similar to those roundly rejected by early Christians faced with mystery religions and gnosticism, it would be ironic to adopt them now. The fact that rationalism has contributed to Europe becoming the most godless piece of the planet is not disputed, but a pendulum-like leap into irrationality is not the right or best response to this sad reality.

The claim that expository preaching is elitist (excluding the vast majority of contemporary people) and authoritarian is also hotly refuted (indeed, some regard the charge of elitism to be, itself, patronising). What is so wrong with attempting to produce a better public level of knowledge about Christianity? Surely this is better than colluding with ignorance and superstition, which is real tyrannical authoritarianism? Expository preaching teaches and preaching has always sought to teach the faith. While it may be the case that few are *brought* into the kingdom because of such preaching, it is equally the case that many *remain* in the kingdom because of it. As far as authoritarianism is concerned, any assertion about divine revelation runs the risk of being misunderstood in this way, and such a charge is par for the course.

The charge that expository preaching is unbiblical is also rejected. The New Testament represents a unique situation, quite different to later generations of Christians charged with delivering 'the faith once delivered to the saints', so one must not read too much into the scarcity of the expository preaching model. Then again, is it so scarce? Are not some of the epistles typical early church sermons bearing many of the hallmarks of good exposition?

Expository preaching, then, must continue to be a part of any Church wishing to remain securely biblical in its ethos. The alternative, arising directly out of relativism, is an anchorless, shapeless, insubstantial Christianity. As David Adam points out, 'Without the Bible the remembered Christ becomes the imagined Christ.' At its best expository preaching attempts to fuse two horizons, the biblical text and the contemporary world, but it *begins* with the biblical text and to abandon this stance would be disastrous.

A defence of expository preaching does not involve the rejection of every aspect of postmodernity. Many expository preachers are convinced that some postmodern themes and concerns will enrich contemporary preaching; for example, the emphasis on intuitive and subjective things is welcome, permitting expository preaching to address the will and the feelings in addition to the mind. So in terms of the challenge to expository preaching itself postmodernity is a threat, but in terms of the openings it gives to explore the purpose of the text more fully, using different criteria, it is an opportunity. In *An Evangelical Theology of Preaching*[2], one of his last books, Donald English introduces and applies a number of insights and methods not found in the traditional 'toolkit' of evangelical Bible expositors while retaining a clear sense of the 'God-givenness' of scripture and its primary place in the preaching enterprise.

Positively postmodern?

At the very least, then, the emergence of postmodern methods of biblical interpretation reminds preachers that they are no longer hidebound by the modernist principles of historical critical methodology, especially when these seem to close down rather than open up effective ways of communicating the gospel to contemporary people. New thoughts can be thought and new methods adopted and the sky will not fall in. It's exciting! I offer a few brief examples.

Influenced by post-critical, postmodern approaches to the Bible some preachers are noting the open-ended nature of scripture and suggesting this is the way God wants it to be. Scripture itself is not all fixed, neatly tied up and fully explainable, and the God to whom it bears witness is most certainly not. How, then, can Christian preaching be so? John Goldingay exemplifies this kind of thinking. He advocates 'scriptural preaching', but by this he does not mean the tedious 'peeling the onion' techniques of various historical critical methods, or preaching strait-jacketed by precise doctrinal formulations. Rather he means preaching that uses methods of communication *that scripture itself uses*. After all, if scripture is God's word, then the methods God uses in communicating with us through it are going to be of significance to Christian preachers. So Goldingay talks of the 'story-shapedness', 'personal-ness' and 'graphic-ness' of scripture, and argues that these elements – of story, especially parables, personal authenticity, and a new, apt form of rhetoric – hold valuable clues for effective Christian communication by preachers in our contemporary cultural context[3]. The form of rhetoric required today is not the links-in-a-chain linear rhetoric of the printed page but the circular, repetitive spiralling oral rhetoric of the televisual era. The repeating of the same point, the repetition of key words, the laying of clear trailers, the introduction of spontaneity and themes not directly arising from the previous point all now hold more promise than a sermon which is a spoken version of a calculated and much revised paper. Never before has hearability been more important and a poorly-read script more potentially damaging. In short, James Logie Baird has replaced Johann Gutenberg and, crucially for Goldingay, these very principles have their roots in scripture itself.

Other writers associate certain aspects of contemporary methods of scriptural interpretation with *pre-modernity* rather than scripture itself. There are new factors most certainly, but there are also clear echoes of how pre-modern Christians understood and applied the scriptures. Jim Jones comments, 'The rich possibilities of post-modern reading methods bear more than passing resemblance to hitherto long-discredited Patristic reading methods.'[4] The net result is the (re)introduction of elements that produce a better balance of subjective and objective factors into the interpretation of scripture. Walter Brueggemann has been a clarion voice urging preachers to be 'poets that speak against a prose world'. In our postmodern context he argues that the task of preaching is to 'open out the good news of the gospel' using alternative modes of speech, speech that 'assaults imagination' and introduces the new life mediated through the 'generative power' of the Bible.[5]

Other writers have suggested principles making for effective oral communication with contemporary people. Jolyon Mitchell suggests that preaching today needs to take on the brevity and directness of speech and the conversational and colloquial styles of oral communication in our increasingly audio-visual culture[6]. It is not enough to provide content; contemporary preaching must also evoke moods. Colin Morris has long asserted the continuing value of good public rhetoric (of which he is himself a master) and urges preachers to take the role of 'public performer' very seriously. He suggests preachers should learn from comedians and actors, particularly in respect of timing, humour, pathos, and emotion[7]. The ability to be conversational and dialogical, even when the only voice speaking at that moment is the preacher's, holds more promise today than the great pulpit oratory of past preaching giants. It is not that such giants were incapable of any of the skills just itemised as much as the fact that contemporary people are likely to be more responsive to preaching that doesn't make them feel preached *at*. This requires the new honing of mainly old skills for a new context. So preaching that is 'living-room' rather than 'classroom', inviting dialogue rather than delivering dogma, conversing with 'each one' rather than addressing 'you all' is the better way in this oral/aural/visual event called a sermon. As with so much postmodern, authenticity and an absence of authoritarianism are crucial.

Two more closely related things arise from the thoughts of these preachers. First, we do well to note the continuing value of insights from historical critical methodology for preaching today. For the vast majority of preachers, preaching remains firmly connected and committed to the 'biblical' and the 'historical'. Second, for increasing numbers of preachers the 'rules' of strict historical critical methodology are not the be-all-and-end-all of preaching. Contemporary preaching brings *past* interpretation and the insights of the Christian Tradition *together with new methods,* producing new insights for today's congregations. Some of these post-critical developments present exciting *opportunities* for Christian preaching and these must not be missed or dismissed. Preachers whose background and training is located firmly in historical critical methods need to note this and loosen up a little!

Preaching the Christian metanarrative . . . revisited

Some of the postmodern criticism of historical critical methodology is well made. The Bible became a scholar's book as they alone had ways of accessing the 'real' meaning and significance of scripture, and consequently it became 'closed' to increasing numbers of 'secular' people, a factor contributing to the widespread ignorance of basic Christianity noted earlier. The dissecting of Bible texts into thousands of bits in order to analyse them in various ways gave rise to valuable and important insights, but also led to a loss of the overall plot. The metanarrative of Christian scripture disappeared, both textually and conceptually. As a result of these undesirable factors preaching has declined as a means of effectively communicating the significance and relevance of scripture to contemporary people. One suggested remedy for this (and one strongly advocated by the Bible Society's *Open Book* project) is the deliberate re-presentation of the Bible *as scripture*, paying particular attention to the remembering and retelling of the overall story – the Christian metanarrative. On this reading of events, therefore, the greater hope lies with *deliberately preaching the Christian metanarrative rather than abandoning it*. In stark terms this sounds decidedly anti-postmodern, even suicidal. In practical terms, as has been hinted earlier, it need not be so. Given the widely acknowledged growth of ignorance in basic Christianity among contemporary people it is worth asking at this point what 'preaching the Christian metanarrative' might mean and what benefits might arise from it.

Lectionaries

It might be argued that 'preaching the Christian metanarrative' means following a lectionary. Certainly a close adherence to, say, the *Revised Common Lectionary* means that enormous amounts of scripture are presented for preaching over a three-year cycle. Yet the contemporary context presents issues that for supporters of the use of lectionaries like myself are deeply challenging and which are unlikely to resolve themselves in the foreseeable future.

For a start all the statistics suggest that fewer and fewer people attend public worship every week, or put more positively, an increasing number of people attend worship every so often. The *Revised Common Lectionary*, like all major lectionaries, was not formulated with such a congregation in mind. The notion of a lectionary first emerged out of settled monastic communities and was then more precisely formulated in the context of the congregations of Christendom. Whether 'continuous', 'semi-continuous' or 'thematic', lectionaries are not at their most effective when applied to here-this-week-but-not-next congregations. As a theoretical mechanism for preaching the biblical metanarrative a good lectionary stands tall; as a *practical* means of relaying the Christian story to contemporary congregations such lectionaries are increasingly being found wanting.

What's to do? Clearly nothing is gained by simply abandoning the use of lectionaries, indeed, individualistic chaos then rules and the chances of the Christian metanarrative being presented virtually disappear. But we are clearly going to have to begin to think new thoughts for a new context. I offer two ideas for the melting pot.

- *Utilising the Christian Year*

First that preachers (and Churches) deliberately commit themselves to maximising the *teaching and evangelistic* opportunities presented in the major points of the *Christian Year*. It has been said that there are two sorts of Christians, those who follow the Christian Year and those who don't. My own Methodist tradition has often played fast and loose in this respect. Only a handful of years ago I went to worship in a village chapel on Easter Day and the preacher announced she felt led to preach on prayer! I want to contend that she shouldn't have felt so led. The Christian Year, beginning at Advent and moving through Christmas and Epiphany, Lent and Easter, Ascension and Pentecost is the most vivid and potentially effective presentation of the Christian metanarrative I know. It is the story of the prehistory, birth, life, teaching, suffering, death, resurrection and ascension of Christ, of the coming of the Holy Spirit and the empowerment for mission and discipleship of the Christian community. It is the Gospel in Time. The Christian Year is a God-given opportunity to present 'the one short tale we feel to be true' with imagination, flair and all five senses. It is deeply human, tremendously transcendent, profoundly mysterious and laden with authentic spirituality. What a postmodern friendly script! What good gospel! A commitment to pour effort and expertise into such occasions of worship is a sound commitment. It reinforces the faithful in the core dimensions of their faith while introducing the seeker and the onlooker to the heart of what and who we are as Christians. Innovative and intelligent, effective and explicit, tangible and tactile ways of calling people to Christian discipleship should be a natural part of every high and holy Day. For it is on these occasions that more than average of the 'floating voters' come along.

- *Working from a reduced canon*

Second, that preachers and Churches consider the more radical suggestion of working from a reduced canon from time to time. Like it or loathe it, the *Alpha Course* represents a success story in terms of introducing 'people on the edge' to Christian faith. It works from a reduced canon; that is, it deliberately chooses what key points from the Christian metanarrative are required initially and provides a defined, short-term context in which they can be presented and discussed. The *Alpha* canon will not be everyone's choice, but that is not the point. I want to urge more preachers in local church settings to consider contextualised canons of the Christian metanarrative for those in front of them. Such short series, particularly if folk are personally invited and accompanied, and even better if the environment is deliberately made 'seeker-sensitive', meet the needs of today's sporadic congregations better than the monolithic notion that a three-year lectionary alone can adequately present Christianity. In the 'lean season' of the Christian Year (often known by the misnomer 'Ordinary Time'), or even as a specific focus of a particular season such as Advent or Lent, short presentations of the Christian metanarrative pay dividends not only for sporadic seekers but also for established Christians.

Making connections

'Preaching the Christian metanarrative' to contemporary congregations will also involve the deliberate *practical application* of biblical texts as much as their exposition. It can be argued that only when the Christian metanarrative *connects* and *intersects* with the lives of contemporary people is it able to be experienced as real and valuable and, therefore, not dismissed so readily as one more bankrupt ideology. The need for sermons to apply the faith rather than simply teach it is not new, and the best notions of exposition always fuse the two, but the postmodern love affair with pragmatism, with 'what works for me', makes it especially important today.

It is necessary to make such an obvious point because the dominance of historical critical methodology has permitted the view that a 'good sermon' is one that merely reproduces the issues with which such methodologies are concerned. Preachers can spend their time informing their congregations who wrote this, when, and why, and this is fine as far as it goes, *but it doesn't go far enough*. Nowadays the 'so what?' is crucial. Some preachers are now saying if you can't 'earth' it, or 'so what it', then don't preach it. Overall – and I know some people hate the word – it leads to preaching which is *irrelevant*, preaching that is *unconnected* to the lives of those in front of us. To teach the Christian faith story without applying it to those in front of you in terms of developing their Christian discipleship is to fall into the trap of limiting Christian preaching to the parameters of much historical criticism. Preaching is not primarily trying to win arguments as much as make disciples, then better disciples of Jesus Christ.

Some aspects of the research undertaken by Mark Greene, referred to in the previous chapter, reinforces these points. Greene asked representatives from almost 100 evangelical churches in the London area what they thought about the preaching they received. The proportion of folk who thought the preaching they heard lacked relevance, depth and challenge is significant. The word 'boring' hardly figured at all but the word 'irrelevant' figured everywhere. Exegesis was not perceived to be the main problem but the preacher's failure to attempt to *apply* biblical exegesis to their lives was. (In fact, some filled in the questionnaire in such a way that they affirmed that a preacher could deliver an 'excellent' sermon that made no connection with their life at all!) Sermons were deemed to be *least* helpful in terms of their life at *work* and at *home* and more helpful in terms of their life in church and their personal Christian discipleship. I note that such preaching bears the marks of long exposure to the modernist view that faith-matters belong to the 'private' rather than 'public' world, and therefore sermons deal fundamentally with the interior life of church rather than the exterior life in the 'world'. I note, too, that Christian preachers in the early Christian centuries would most likely have disowned such limited preaching on the basis that it neither produced mature Christians nor truly represented Christianity to those who did not yet belong to it. Which are, of course, precisely the shortcomings of such stunted preaching today.

Picking up an earlier theme I want to contend that preaching that seeks to connect and apply the Christian big story rather than simply teach it is better for *all concerned*, 'believers' and 'seekers' alike. It helps Christians in their growth and discipleship by rooting that growth in the 'world' not the church, in whole-life, holistic discipleship rather than spiritual schizophrenia. In our contemporary cultural context such Christians will be better authentic witnesses to their faith than if they remain 'ghettoised'. Therefore, even if preachers have only converted folk in their congregations (which is highly unlikely), preaching that connects and applies is better than what many feel they are receiving at the moment. That contemporary Christians themselves are desirous of such preaching is most encouraging and a salutary word to preachers who tell us everything in their congregational garden is rosy.

Although Greene's research dealt with regular church-attending Christians rather than 'occasional seekers' it is hard not to come to the conclusion that preaching that connects and applies rather than simply teaches is better for these folk too. A privatised, irrelevant Christian ideology will remain easily rejected for many contemporary people, and preachers who present Christianity in such terms will have a steady throughput of those who sample then continue to look elsewhere. An engaging, wrestling-with-real-life, authentic head and heart faith, which connects to human life, living and lifestyle, will certainly challenge postmodern people at a variety of points, and represents a Christian metanarrative that is not so easily rejected.

'Spiritual' preaching for spiritual people

Those who responded to Mark Greene's questionnaire, and laid the charge that preaching was irrelevant, shallow and unchallenging, pose an important question about the kind of preaching and preacher likely to be most effective in our postmodern, post-Christian context. Many suggestions have been made in the preceding pages and do not require repetition here. One final theme outlined in chapter three demands to be briefly revisited, however, and that concerns the issue of spirituality. Given the interest in spirituality and mystery amongst contemporary people, however much some 'sniff' at its nature, we must note the potential significance of preachers incarnating an attractive *Christian* spirituality and regularly engaging in 'spiritual preaching'.

For many preachers 'spiritual preaching' will not come easy. John Drane has pointed out the irony that many postmodern, post-Christian people have rejected Christianity and its Church because they do not consider it spiritual enough.[8]   Previous generations of 'modern' people rejecting Christianity on the basis that it was 'religious' made some sort of sense, today's rejection of Christianity by postmodern people on the basis that it is not religious enough begs all sorts of questions of us. While biblical scholars were busy demythologising the Bible, it appears the world was busy being re-mythologised in a variety of ways.   Christian preachers became disenchanted just as large numbers of Western people got tired of all that and opted for enchantment. Alister Hardy and David Hay have made quite clear the extent to which 'spiritual' experiences are the normal lot of a vast proportion of people today.   The rational inheritance of modernity has not encouraged open, mysterious,   transcendent,   profound,   awe-filled spirituality, yet our contemporary context calls us to cease being embarrassed with the mystical and numinous and invites us to focus more on these things. We reject that call at our peril.

Debra Washington talks of 'God doing the work in us' before we preach it, and then preaching it in a way that makes plain God has done the work in us. She talks of being 'pregnant with the word God is giving'.[9] Perhaps the growing number of women preachers will enable us to refocus on profoundly moving and attractive spiritual aspects of our faith?   It is clear that preaching that is earthed, conversant with human suffering, not trite or clinical about unfathomable questions, full of imagination, mystery and images, and which gives physical expression to spiritual reality, communicates at a deep level to many people today.   We must become more authentically spiritual. In this, as in all things, God's Spirit will help us.

Final 'call'

John Wesley's famous decision to become 'more vile' essentially concerned preaching. It was a decision made in response to a question which burned in his spirit: 'How shall I preach the Christian gospel to those in front of me?'

His 'vile' decision was to preach outdoors, away from the pulpits of the Established Church of England, in order to declare the gospel to the 'ordinary' folk of 18th century Britain, folk largely estranged from the Christian gospel and the Christian Church. In making this decision Wesley rejected inherited notions of respectability, decency and 'holiness', and refuted the accepted ways of preaching – hence the 'vileness'. Making the decision took time, did not come easy, and required openness, faith, courage and commitment. Yet, once taken, the decision did not lack God's resources or anointing. However vile it was, the decision was the right one.

Wesley's context is not ours, yet the same burning question faces Christian preachers today: how shall we preach the Christian gospel to the postmodern, post-Christian people in front of us? The answers may well fly in the face of various inherited notions of preaching. They will certainly not come easily and will indeed take time, openness, faith, courage and commitment. Yet the call to be 'more vile' is before us and is, as it was for Wesley, a gospel call. Like Wesley, those who respond to such a call will not lack God's resources and anointing.

NOTES

Chapter 1

1. Michael Green, *Evangelism in the Early Church*, (London, Hodder & Stoughton, 1970) p.70.

2. P T Forsyth, *Positive Preaching and the Modern Mind*, (Carlisle, Paternoster Press, 1998) p.5. (First published in 1907.)

Chapter 2

1. See Andrew F Walls, *The Missionary Movement in Christian History*, (Edinburgh, T&T Clark, 1996) p.7ff.

2. Louis J Luzbetak, *The Church and Cultures*, (Maryknoll, Orbis, 1988) p.134.

3. 2 Corinthians 5:1f.

4. *Phillips Brooks on Preaching*, (London, SPCK, 1965) p.19-20.

Chapter 3

1. Michael Paul Gallagher SJ, *Clashing Symbols*, (London, Darton, Longman and Todd, 1997) p.87.

2. Zygmunt Bauman, 'Postmodernity, or Living with Ambivalence' in *Modernity and Ambivalence*, (Oxford, Blackwell, 1991).

3. *Cit.* David Hilborn, *Picking up the Pieces*, (London, Hodder & Stoughton, 1997) pp.26 & 32.

4. Graham Cray, 'Postmodernity – under construction', in *The Gospel and our Culture Network Newsletter*, Spring, 2000. (The Bible Society.)

5. Grace Davie's book is subtitled 'Believing without Belonging', (Oxford, Blackwell, 1994).

6. For example, Steve Bruce, *Religion in the Modern World*, (Oxford University Press, 1996).

7. George Hunter III, *How to Reach Secular People*, (Nashville, Abingdon Press, 1992) *passim*.

8. Martin Robinson, *The Faith of the Unbeliever*, (Crowborough, Monarch, 1994) p.93.

Chapter 4

1. Harry L Poe, 'Making the Most of Postmodernity', *Journal of the Academy for Evangelism in Theological Education*, Vol. 13, 1997-1998. P.67ff.

2. See, for example, Willimon's *Peculiar Speech: Preaching to the Baptized* and *The Intrusive Word: Preaching to the Unbaptized*, (Grand Rapids, Eerdmans, 1992 & 1994).

Chapter 5

1. Often stated by Newbigin, and a theme taken up in some detail in *The Gospel in a Pluralist Society*, (London, SPCK, 1989).

2. Donald English, *Into the 21st Century*, (Methodist Church Home Mission, 1995) *passim*.

3. *Cit.* Andrew Walker, *Telling the Story* (London, SPCK, 1996) p.5.

4. Stephen Toulmin, *Cosmopolis*: *The Hidden Agenda of Modernity*, (New York, Free Press, 1990) pp.186-192.

5. A phrase Walker repeatedly employs in his fine book, *Telling the Story.*

6. Mark Greene, 'Is Anybody Listening' in *Anvil*, Vol. 14 No.4 1997 and the lead article in *Quadrant*, November 1998, published by *Christian Research*.

7. *The Gospel in a Pluralist Society*, p.232, but read all chapter 18.

Chapter 6

1. The material in this section draws extensively from: Roy Clements, 'Expository preaching in a postmodern world', *Cambridge Papers*, vol. 7, no.3, September 1998.

2. Donald English, *An Evangelical Theology of Preaching*, (Nashville, Abingdon Press, 1996).

3. John Goldingay, 'In Preaching be Scriptural', *Anvil*, vol.14, no.2, 1997, pp.87ff.

4. Jim W Jones, 'Ancient and Post-modern Reading of Scripture', *The College of Preachers Fellowship Paper*, No 105, June 1998, p.24.

5. See, for example, the Introduction and Chapter 2 of Brueggemann's *Abiding Astonishment*, (Minneapolis, Fortress Press, 1989).

6. Jolyon Mitchell, 'Preaching in an Audio-Visual Culture', *Anvil*, vol.14, no.4, 1997, pp.262ff.

7. Colin Morris, *Raising the Dead*, (London, Fount, 1996).

8. See, for example, John Drane, *Faith in a Changing Culture*, (London, Marshall Pickering, 1997).

9. Taped lectures at a Cliff College Conference, 'The Art of Preaching' 1997.